Digital Video

SAMS

A Division of Macmillan USA
201 West 103rd Street
Indianapolis, Indiana 46290

Dave Johnson

Visually in **Full Color**

How to Use Digital Video

International Standard Book Number: 0-672-31923-3

Library of Congress Catalog Card Number: 00-102115

Printed in the United States of America

First Printing: July 2000

03   02   01   00   4   3   2   1

Trademarks

All terms mentioned in this book that are known to be trademarks or service marks have been appropriately capitalized. Sams Publishing cannot attest to the accuracy of this information. Use of a term in this book should not be regarded as affecting the validity of any trademark or service mark.

Warning and Disclaimer

Every effort has been made to make this book as complete and as accurate as possible, but no warranty or fitness is implied. The information provided is on an "as is" basis. The author and the publisher shall have neither liability nor responsibility to any person or entity with respect to any loss or damages arising from the information contained in this book or from the use of the CD or programs accompanying it.

Executive Editor
Randi Roger

Acquisitions Editor
Elizabeth Brown

Development Editor
Alice Martina Smith

Managing Editor
Charlotte Clapp

Project Editor
Carol Bowers

Copy Editor
Mike Henry

Indexer
Eric Schroeder

Proofreader
Katherin Bidwell

Technical Editor
Alan Hamill

Interior Designers
Nathan Clement
Ruth Lewis

Cover Designers
Nathan Clement
Aren Howell

Layout Technicians
Ayanna Lacey
Heather Hiatt Miller
Mark Walchle

Contents at a Glance

Contents

About the Author

Dave Johnson writes about technology from his home in Colorado Springs, Colorado. He's a Senior Editor at Planet IT, a contributing editor at *Home Office Computing*, and writes frequently for magazines such as *Working Mother Magazine* and *Family PC*. He's the author of more than a dozen books that include *Digital Photography Answers* and *How to Do Everything with Your Palm Handheld* (with Rick Broida).

Dave started writing professionally in 1990, before anyone had a chance to talk him out of it. Before that, he had a somewhat unfocused career that included flying satellites, driving an ice cream truck, managing weapons at an Air Force base, stocking shelves at Quick Check, teaching rocket science, photographing a rock band, and writing about space penguins. He's still not playing bass in a psychedelic band, but at least he's found steady work.

Acknowledgements

Acknowledgements are usually the part of the book in which authors pander to various people by insisting that the acknowledgements in the last book were just plain obsequious, but this time they really, really mean it.

Well, I'm here to say that regardless of what I wrote in my last book, this time I really, really mean it. *Really!* And I'll tell you why: When **Randi Roger** and I first started talking about creating a digital video book, she gave me unprecedented control over the look and feel of the book. She asked me to help create a visual design that would be different from the typical *How to Use* book and really helped me tell the story that I wanted to write. I drew sketches on napkins and faxed them to Randi, and she took them and turned my scrawls into real page layouts. And when I whined that they didn't quite "realize my artistic vision" of the book, she revised them again. I can't thank Randi enough for her dedication to this project.

And Randi wasn't the only one at Macmillan who was helping drive this title forward. Many thanks also go to **Alice Martina Smith, Amy Patton, Betsy Brown**, and everyone who made the totally cool line art and page designs for this book.

Thanks also go to **Neil Salkind** and the crew at **Studio B**. I'm still waiting for the Letterman gig.

Thanks to the great folks at Adobe and MGI for assisting with the book as well. Special thanks go to **Shelly Sofer** and **Alan Hamill**.

I can't imagine writing a book without the sound of **Kristin Hersh** in the background. Kristin, thanks for creating music that speaks directly to me.

Finally, my friends and family deserve a medal. **Kris, Evan**, and **Marin**, I love you all.

Dedication

For Kevin, Anne, Christine, and Shadow.

Tell Us What You Think!

As the reader of this book, *you* are our most important critic and commentator. We value your opinion and want to know what we're doing right, what we could do better, what areas you'd like to see us publish in, and any other words of wisdom you're willing to pass our way.

You can fax, email, or write directly to let me know what you did or didn't like about this book—as well as what we can do to make our books stronger.

Please note that I cannot help you with technical problems related to the topic of this book, and that because of the high volume of mail I receive, I might not be able to reply to every message.

When you write, please be sure to include this book's title and author as well as your name and phone or fax number. I will carefully review your comments and share them with the author and editors who worked on the book.

Fax: 317-581-4770

Email: `graphics_sams@mcp.com`

Mail: Mark Taber
Associate Publisher
Sams Publishing
201 West 103rd Street
Indianapolis, IN 46290 USA

How to Use This Book

The Complete Visual Reference

Each part of this book is made up of a series of short, instructional tasks, designed to help you understand all the information you need to get the most out of your digital video projects.

Click: Click the left mouse button once.

Double-click: Click the left mouse button twice in rapid succession.

Right-click: Click the right mouse button once.

Pointer Arrow: Highlights an item on the screen you need to point to or focus on in the step or task.

Selection: This circle highlights the area that is discussed in the step.

Keyboard: Type information or data into the indicated location.

Background colors and special highlighted steps in VideoWave and Premiere.

Each task includes a series of easy-to-understand steps designed to guide you through the procedure.

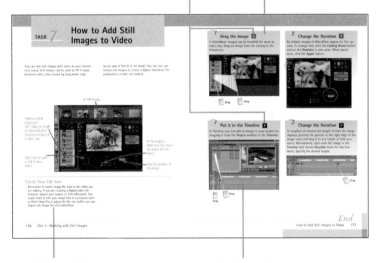

Extra hints that tell you how to accomplish a goal are provided in most tasks.

Each step is fully illustrated to show you how to do the task.

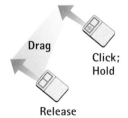

Drag

Click; Hold

Release

Drag and drop: Position the mouse pointer over the object, click and hold the left mouse button, drag the object to its new location, and release the mouse button.

Screen elements (such as menus, icons, windows, and so on), as well as things you enter or select, appear in **boldface** type.

continues

If you see this symbol, it means that the task or project you're in continues on the next page.

Introduction

*D*igital video is exciting. Imagine this: Using a camcorder, you can create a movie. Then you can transfer the video to your PC, where—without losing one tiny scrap of resolution—you can rearrange the scenes, add music, include transitions, overlay titles, and add special effects. When you're done, you can output the completed masterpiece back to videotape. Or upload the movie to the Internet. Or burn a copy onto CD-ROM.

Editing video on the computer used to be complicated and expensive. Not anymore. The advent of digital video (DV) camcorders and a set of standards for getting the data into and out of your PC now makes video editing accessible to everyone. The best part is that in years past, editing video was destructive to the video itself. Every time you made a copy of a copy of the video—which is necessary to assemble scenes and overlay titles—the quality degraded. DV preserves your image quality through the entire process, so what you end up with is just the same as what you started with. What's cooler than that?

In This Book

So, you want to create your own videos, but where do you start? That's where this book comes in. I wrote *How to Use Digital Video* as a comprehensive roadmap to doing everything from using your camcorder to capturing video into the PC to editing and publishing your finished work. That means I don't leave anything out—I think this is the most complete book on video you can buy.

And each task is explained in a step-by-step fashion, complete with pictures to help you do it yourself. By the time you're done with this book, you should be able to do all of these things, plus much more:

✓ Shoot video under a variety of lighting conditions

✓ Create a complete movie with multiple scenes, transitions, and titles

✓ Add complex, multisource audio to your movie soundtracks

✓ Output your movie to videotape

✓ Publish streaming video movies to the Internet using RealPlayer

✓ Add video to PowerPoint presentations

There are many video-editing programs available, but I have two favorites: Adobe Premiere 5.1 and MGI VideoWave III. As a consequence, you'll find that this book is unique: I show you how to do most video projects using both programs! I assume that you're using VideoWave most of the time—it's an easy program to use, and a good one to learn the basics of video editing with. Because there are certain advanced techniques you can't do very well or at all with VideoWave, I also offer you Premiere. If you later decide to use Premiere all the time because of its greater power, you've already got a guide to that program—this book! And don't worry, you won't get confused about which program this book refers to; you can always tell by the color of the background whether you're looking at a VideoWave or a Premiere step. We also use a Premiere **P** icon and a VideoWave **V** icon to help differentiate the steps in the tasks that refer to both programs. If you don't care about Premiere, ignore those **P** steps, at least for now.

So, go get started. The first part of the book is a roadmap of sorts. Check it out to see all the steps in the video production process laid out for you. To see a step explained in detail, just turn to the appropriate part of the book. You can also get a sneak peek at the major parts of Premiere, VideoWave, and a typical camcorder in Part 1. From there, where you go is up to you.

If you run into questions that aren't addressed in this book, you can always contact me for additional information. Visit my Web site at www.radioguys.com or email me at dvquestions@radioguys.com. I'll do my best to answer your questions—and your comments might be integrated into the next version of this book.

Good luck with your next video!

Task

Getting Started

*W*elcome to the exciting world of digital video! Using your camcorder, a PC, and some editing software, you can now create movies that rival the kind of stuff you see on television. The problem is knowing exactly where to start. That's why I've tried to make it easy—in this part of the book, I've created some roadmaps for you. Start with the Video Production Roadmap. There, you'll find every major step along the path to video production laid out in snapshot form. Not only can you see the major steps along the way to making your first movie, you can also see where in the book you can turn for detailed instructions.

Before you go any further, grab the CD-ROM from the back of the book and install the software you're going to need to make videos. The disc includes my favorite video editors—MGI VideoWave and Adobe Premiere—and I've written the book in such a way that you can, for the most part, use either of these excellent programs to edit and produce movies on the PC. The disc also includes a bunch of other great tools, such as Adobe After Effects and Jasc's Paint Shop Pro. Follow the steps in Task 3 to install the software from the CD.

After that, you can check out guided tours of a typical digital camcorder along with VideoWave and Premiere. These tours show you the major interface elements of the programs so that you can dive right into the step-by-step instructions in the rest of the book.

A Video Production Roadmap

Video editing isn't as complicated as it might seem. Sure, there are a lot of things to learn—but you had to master your word processor once, too. In the next few pages, I lay out all the major ingredients in making a video. Follow along for a sneak peek at what this book has to offer.

1 Create a Plan

Your plan—called a *storyboard* in video parlance—helps you decide what video to shoot and how to assemble all the video clips into a single video production. **Part 2, Task 1, "How to Use a Storyboard."**

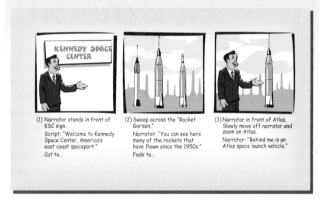

(1) Narrator stands in front of KSC sign.
Script: "Welcome to Kennedy Space Center, America's east coast spaceport."
Cut to...

(2) Sweep across the "Rocket Garden."
Narrator: "You can see here many of the rockets that have flown since the 1950s."
Fade to...

(3) Narrator in front of Atlas. Slowly move off narrator and zoom on Atlas.
Narrator: "Behind me is an Atlas space launch vehicle."

2 Have Enough Memory

Make sure that your computer has enough memory, or your video may be jittery, since the computer runs out of RAM and has to use the hard disk's slower swap file to generate video frames. **Part 3, Task 1, "How to Install More Memory."**

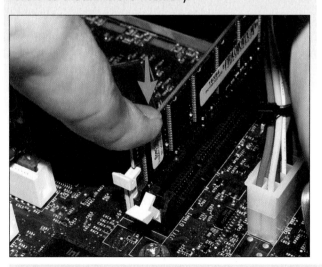

3 How Big Is Your Hard Drive?

You'll need about 250MB of hard drive space for every minute of video you shoot. Is your hard drive big enough? If not, get a new one. **Part 3, Task 2, "How to Install a New Hard Drive."**

4 Install a Video Capture Card

You need a video capture card that's compatible with your editing software and with the kind of camcorder you are using. **Part 3, Task 3, "How to Install a Video Capture Card."**

5 Start Shooting

Load the film in your camcorder, perform a white balance to ensure that you've got good color balance in your video, and start shooting! **Part 2, Tasks 2 and 7, "How to Handle DV Tapes," and "How to White-Balance Your Scene."**

6 Capture Video

Then you'll have to grab the video from your camcorder and "capture" it into your PC before you can start editing the video. **Part 3, Task 5, "How to Capture Video."**

7 Organize Your Movie

Organize all the video clips you've just captured to your hard drive by referring to your storyboard and dragging your clips to the video Storyline. **Part 4, Task 2, "How to Populate the Storyline."**

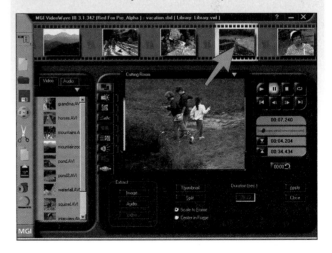

continues

A Video Production Roadmap Continued

8 Trim Your Video

Fine-tune your clips by trimming the fat. Your clips should be sharp, focused, and to the point. **Part 4, Task 5, "How to Trim the Length of a Clip."**

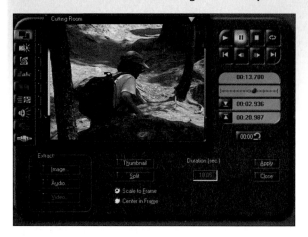

9 Grab Still Frames

Take snapshots of scenes in your movie or import photographs into your video to give some variety and additional interest to the final production. **Part 7, Tasks 1 and 7, "How to Capture an Image from Video," and "How to Add Still Images to Video."**

10 Capture CD Audio

Grab music from CDs and insert the audio tracks into your movie. Note that copyright laws prohibit you from using commercial sound tracks in anything other than a video intended for personal use. **Part 6, Task 1, "How to Capture a Song from CD."**

11 Mix Sound

Add sound from narration, music, and other sources into your movie's soundtrack. **Part 6, Task 4, "How to Mix Audio Tracks."**

12 Fixing Audio Glitches

Your audio and video don't always line up perfectly. Engineer the sound so that it all looks and sounds great. **Part 6, Tasks 7 and 8, "How to Extend Video to Match Audio," and "How to Create an Audio Transition."**

13 Add Transitions

Transitions can be an elegant way to move from one scene to another. Choose from wipes, fades, and dozens of other effects—but use transitions in moderation. **Part 4, Task 7, "How to Add a Transition Between Scenes."**

14 Add Titles

Overlay titles on video or on color panels. Create titles, subtitles, and captions to help identify your video to your viewers. **Part 5, Task 1, "How to Add Titles to a Video."**

15 Add Special Effects

Overlay a video clip on top of another clip for very cool results! **Part 4, Task 10, "How to Superimpose Video."**

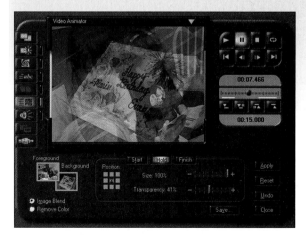

continues

A Video Production Roadmap   **9**

A Video Production Roadmap Continued

16 Create a Video Slideshow

Synchronize music and still images as a slideshow interlude in the middle of your video. **Project 2, "Creating a Video Slide Show."**

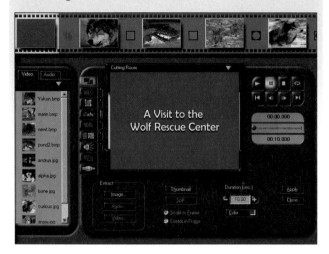

17 Roll the Credits

Add rolling credits to the end of your video production to identify all those involved in the film or just to have the final word. **Part 5, Task 5, "How to Make Credits Roll."**

18 Preview Your Production

At any point in the production, you can preview your creation on the computer screen to get a rough idea of what it will look like when done. **Part 4, Task 16, "How to Preview Your Movie on the Computer."**

19 Produce the Movie

When the production is complete, generate the finished movie file. **Part 8, Task 1, "How to Prepare Your Video for Tape."**

20 Copy It to Videotape

Create a videotape from your produced movie file. **Part 8, Task 2, "How to Copy the Finished Video to Tape."**

21 Put It on the Web

Take small movie files and upload them to a Web page where anyone can appreciate them. **Part 9, Tasks 1, 2, and 3, "How to Prepare Your Video for the Web," "How to Insert a Movie Into a Web Page," and "How to Upload the Movie to the Web."**

22 Burn a CD-ROM

Copy your video to CD and distribute it just as you would a digital videotape. **Part 9, Task 6, "How to Put Your Video on CD-ROM."**

23 Insert Video into PowerPoint

Take your video clips and insert them into a presentation in PowerPoint. **Part 10, Task 2, "How to Insert Video into PowerPoint."**

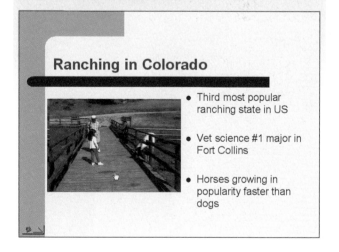

End

How to Get Around Your Camcorder

No two camcorders are exactly alike, but they tend to share many things in common. I've used this very popular JVC CyberCam to point out the most important features of whatever camcorder you use. Shooting clips using a digital camcorder is the same as using an analog camera; the differences generally become apparent only when you are transferring video from the camera to the PC. With a digital

camcorder, you transfer video digitally with a FireWire connector; older VHS or 8mm camcorders need an analog capture card (see Part 3, Task 3 for more info on that). Familiarize yourself with the features and controls of your camera so that when you're actually shooting video, you won't have to interrupt the shoot to find the zoom feature of your camera.

LCD display for filming and playback.

Optical viewfinder.

Tape playback controls.

Power controls.

Speaker for playback.

Zoom lens.

Battery.

Video light.

Microphone.

1 Inputs

DV camcorders connect to the PC with a FireWire connector, also known as IEEE1394. If you have an analog camcorder, you'll use composite audio and video cables instead.

2 Menu Controls

When your camera is in Manual mode, you can access the onscreen menus by pressing the menu dial and turning it.

3 Inside the Viewscreen

Menus are displayed on the LCD viewscreen and in the viewfinder.

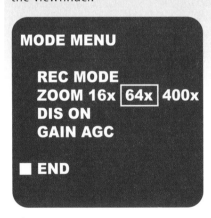

4 Tripod Connector

Most camcorders have a threaded socket in the bottom of the camera for attaching a tripod. You should use a tripod in low-light conditions or when panning an action scene to eliminate the shake that's typical when you hold the camera in your hand.

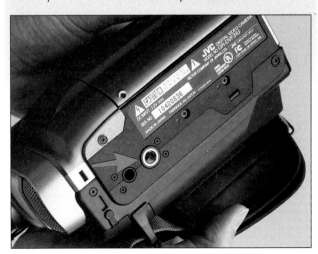

End

How to Install Software from the CD-ROM

I envisioned this book as a complete video editing tool that not only included lessons on editing, but also featured whatever software you'd need to get started. In fact, because the book includes both VideoWave and Premiere, it has a built-in upgrade path when you're ready for more video-production power. In addition to the two editors, the disc at the back of this book also includes the other software we use later in the book (Jasc's Paint Shop Pro and Real Network's RealProducer). The disc even includes some bonus software you can experiment with (such as Adobe After Effects). The only thing I couldn't throw in is the camcorder! Follow the steps in this task to install the software from the CD-ROM and get organized to start working with video.

Free forever.

Description of application.

Click here to install application.

Click here to reset Web resources.

Install a Web browser.

Register to get more cool stuff.

Contact us if you have problems.

Application works only for a limited time; then you must buy it to continue using it.

Organize Your Files

You should be very deliberate about managing the video, sound, and still image files on your hard drive. These files tend to be large, and you won't want to lose track of them. I recommend that you dedicate an entire hard disk to your video files—get a fast Ultra ATA/33 or Ultra ATA/66 hard drive (which I discuss in Part 3, Task 4 of the book). As for the other files, I suggest that you store images in the **My Pictures** folder; store sound files in the **My Music** folder on your C: drive. This way, you'll always know how to find your files quickly and easily.

1 Insert the Disc in the Drive

Carefully remove the CD-ROM from the back of the book and place it in your CD-ROM drive.

2 Display the Installation Menu

A few moments after you insert the disc, the computer should autostart the disc, and you'll see the CD-ROM interface. If you don't, double-click the **My Computer** icon on the Windows desktop and then double-click the CD-ROM drive icon. Then double-click the icon called **START.EXE**.

3 Install VideoWave

The first program you should install on your hard drive is MGI VideoWave (it will be near the bottom of the list). To do that, click the **Software Library** button, then click the **View Software Library** button that appears in the middle of the screen. Find VideoWave in the list of applications and select it.

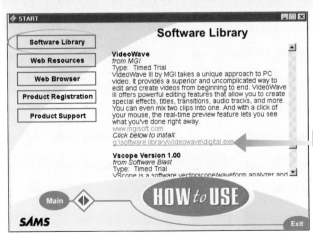

Click

4 Follow the Install Wizard

Follow the instructions onscreen to install VideoWave on your PC. Unless you have a good reason not to, accept the default install location, which will be `C:\program files\mgi`.

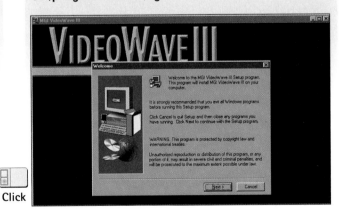

continues

How to Install Software from the CD-ROM   15

5 Install More Software

When the VideoWave installation is complete, add any other programs you want. If you're short on hard disk space, you can skip installing Premiere and After Effects, at least for now. You should definitely install Paint Shop Pro, however. If you plan to create streaming Webcasts of your movies, install the RealProducer software.

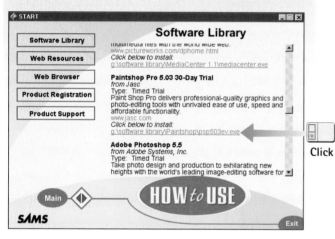

6 Surf the Web

When you're done installing software, you might want to explore the other features on the disc. In particular, be sure to check out related Web sites by clicking the **Web Resources** button.

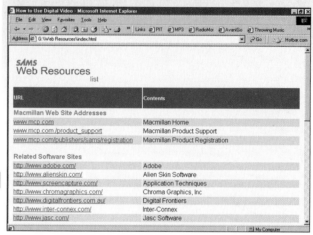

Click

7 Restart Now

After all your software is installed, remove the CD-ROM from the drive and return it to the back of the book (or file it somewhere for safekeeping). Make sure that there are no floppy disks in your PC's floppy drive and restart your PC by choosing **Start, Restart**.

Click

8 Configure the Second Hard Disk

As explained later in the book, I highly recommend that you use a separate hard disk for storing your camcorder's video clips. If you don't have a second hard disk ready now, go buy one and install it (see Part 3, Task 2, "How to Install a New Hard Drive"). If you don't plan to get a second hard disk, you can still edit video, but your results may not be optimal.

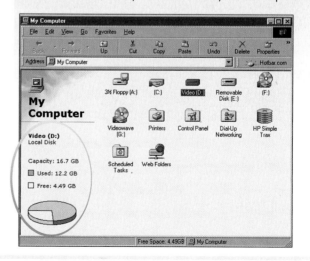

9 Start VideoWave

Now we'll tell VideoWave to use that second hard disk for processing video. Start MGI VideoWave by choosing **Start, MGI VideoWave III, MGI VideoWave III**.

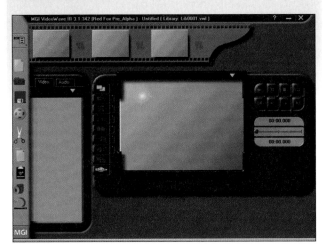

10 Display the Capture Mode

Click the **Capture** button at the bottom of the column of icons (to the left of the Viewscreen).

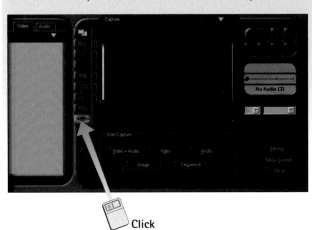

Click

11 Open the Capture Preferences

Click the **Settings** button, and you'll see the **Capture Settings** dialog box. On the **Source** tab, click the **Preferences** button to display the **Capture Preferences** dialog box.

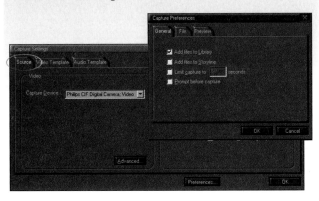

12 Set the Hard Disk Location

In the **Capture Preferences** dialog box, click the **File** tab. Set the **Capture Directory** option to a folder in your dedicated video hard drive (which should be a fast Ultra ATA/33 or Ultra ATA/66 hard drive with plenty of space—no less than 10GB). Click **OK** to close all the dialog boxes.

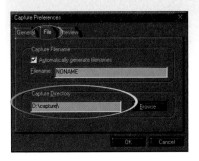

End

How to Install Software from the CD-ROM   17

How to Get Around MGI VideoWave III

VideoWave is a great program because it has perhaps 80% of the most important features in a high-end program such as Adobe Premiere, yet it's easy to learn and almost impossible to "get lost" in. VideoWave uses a Storyline at the top of the screen for arranging your clips, a library on the left side of the screen, and a multipurpose editing room in the middle. The function of the middle of the screen changes depending on what mode you're in.

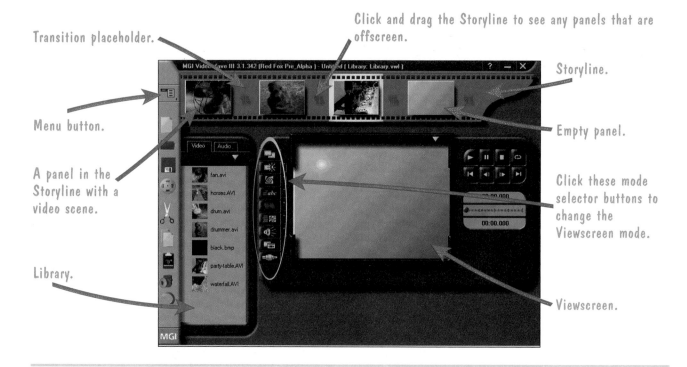

Click and drag the Storyline to see any panels that are offscreen.

Transition placeholder.

Menu button.

A panel in the Storyline with a video scene.

Library.

Storyline.

Empty panel.

Click these mode selector buttons to change the Viewscreen mode.

Viewscreen.

File Formats

You'll see a variety of file formats when you edit video in programs such as VideoWave and Premiere, and some of them might be new to you. Here are the most common formats:

AVI The Video for Windows format is commonly used as the "delivery method" for playing video on a Windows PC. Your finished movies will often be in this format.

MPG The MPG (or MPEG) format is a great video format when you're playing back from the Web or CD-ROM because it highly compresses your movie.

WAV The WAV format is a common way of encoding and playing sound files.

MP3 MP3s are a relatively new audio format, most commonly used to copy songs from audio CDs.

TIF TIF is a high-quality format for still images.

JPG The JPG (or JPEG) format is a great format for displaying still images on the Web because it compresses the file size significantly while having minimal effect on image quality.

1 Accessing the Menus

VideoWave has several menus, but they're not in a menu bar at the top of the screen as you might expect. Instead, the main menu is found by clicking the menu button at the top left of the screen. Other menus are indicated by the arrowheads that point down at the Library and Viewscreen.

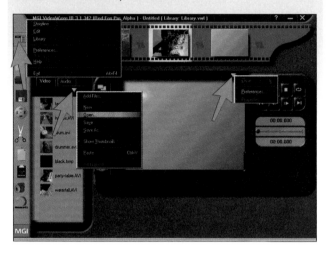

2 Controlling Effects

Many elements in your videos can change during the course of a scene. Click the **Start** button to set the initial conditions of the scene; the **Hold** button lets you set what happens in the middle of the scene; the **Finish** button sets the conditions for the end of the scene.

3 Control Effect Timing

You can control not just the effect itself, but the timing of the **Start**, **Hold**, and **Finish** effects. The four buttons under the slider let you "punch-in" the point at which the effect starts and ends, as well as when and how long the hold effect occurs. To avoid an extended hold period but to move smoothly from start to finish, click the **Hold Start** and **Hold Finish** buttons at the same point in the timeline.

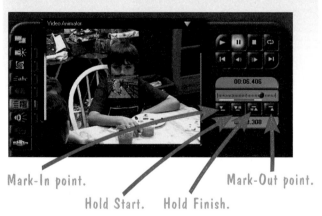

Mark-In point. Mark-Out point.

Hold Start. Hold Finish.

4 VCR Controls

If you need to play a video clip, use the VCR controls to control the video. The buttons do just what you'd expect them to do if you found them on a cassette tape player—only now, you're playing video clips.

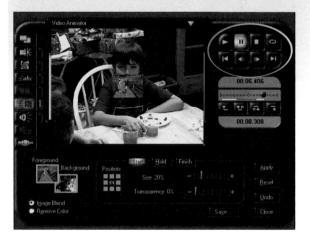

End

How to Get Around Adobe Premiere 5.1

Throughout this book, I've included alternative steps that involve Premiere instead of VideoWave. I did that for two reasons: First, it's an easy way to learn both programs at the same time. Second, there are effects I wanted to teach you that are simply impossible to do in VideoWave, but are easily accomplished in Premiere. So, this book is two for the price of one: When you're ready to step up to Premiere, you've already got a handy guide.

The **Source Monitor** plays video clips.

The **Target Monitor** plays the movie.

The **Project** window holds the clips.

Each clip has an audio and a video track.

Transitions have a special track.

Transitions window.

You can change the magnification of the Timeline.

Set Premiere's Workspace

Back in Task 3, I showed you how to set VideoWave to record and edit video on a specific hard disk. You should do the same in Premiere. Start the program and choose **File, Preferences, Scratch Disks/Device Control**. From the dialog box that appears, choose your fastest hard disk (preferably a dedicated drive) for your video work.

Premiere Steps Identified

P To help you identify instructions in this book that are for Adobe Premiere, the background color for the steps changes and the icon appears next to the step heading. If you don't see these cues, the instructions are for MGI VideoWave.

1 Configuring Your Project P

When you first start Premiere, you should configure the program to use the right settings for the kind of movie you plan to make. Choose an appropriate compressor in the series of **Project Settings** dialog boxes, for instance, as well as the proper frame size for your movie. (Click **Prev** and **Next** to move between the pages of this dialog box.)

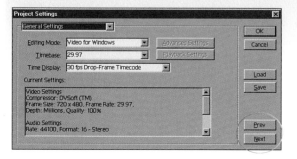

2 Displaying Windows P

You can close windows you aren't using in Premiere, but you need to know how to get them open again. Choose **Window** from the menu bar; you'll find the **Project**, **Monitor**, **Timeline**, and **Transition** windows there.

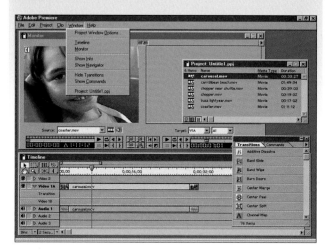

3 The Timeline P

Unlike VideoWave's Storyline, the Premiere Timeline lets you add clips one after another in tracks (the default track is **Video 1A**). To perform special effects such as superimposing video and adding transitions, you add clips on alternate tracks. There can be up to 99 video tracks and an additional 99 audio tracks available for each clip in Premiere.

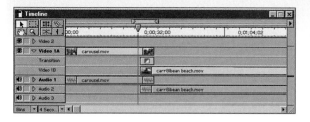

4 Trimming Clips P

The **Source Monitor** window contains controls for locating specific frames of video and marking them as the start and end of the scene. An **Apply** button appears over the clip. Click the **Apply** button to save the edits and update the scene in the Timeline.

End

Task

PART 2

Working with Your Camcorder

*B*efore you can start editing your video like a digital version of a Steven Spielberg blockbuster film, you must first create your video footage. For that, you must become familiar with your camcorder and learn how to get the most out of it.

Modern camcorders are wonders of automation; in general, all you need to do to get acceptable results is press the red Record button and start filming. But there's a lot more you can do to knock the socks off your audience. By mastering the manual controls on your camera, you can create video that is noticeably better. If you plan ahead, you can optimize your footage for the movie you plan to piece together eventually on your PC.

The tasks in this part of the book help you learn to plan the video you have to shoot to ultimately create the movie. You'll learn about some of the basic features of most of today's camcorders as well as some simple props and techniques you can use to improve the quality of the video you shoot. You don't have to be a member of an Oscar-award–winning film crew to get great results, but you should be familiar with the techniques presented in the following tasks. ●

How to Use a Storyboard

Most film projects benefit from a bit of planning and preparation. One of the first things you should do when you set out to make a video is to storyboard it.

A *storyboard* describes the events of the film in thumbnail form. You'll find a storyboard handy for staying on track and on schedule.

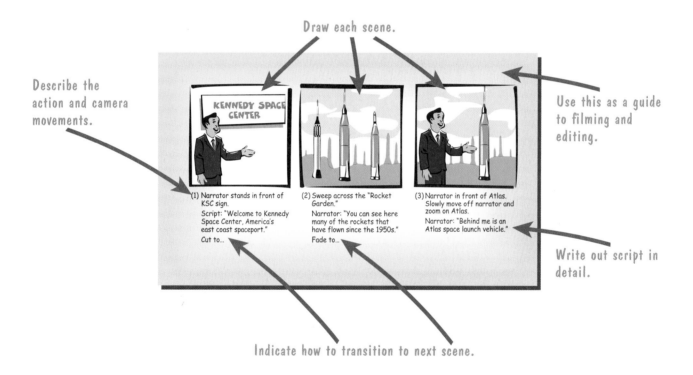

Draw each scene.

Describe the action and camera movements.

Use this as a guide to filming and editing.

(1) Narrator stands in front of KSC sign.
Script: "Welcome to Kennedy Space Center, America's east coast spaceport."
Cut to...

(2) Sweep across the "Rocket Garden."
Narrator: "You can see here many of the rockets that have flown since the 1950s."
Fade to...

(3) Narrator in front of Atlas. Slowly move off narrator and zoom on Atlas.
Narrator: "Behind me is an Atlas space launch vehicle."

Write out script in detail.

Indicate how to transition to next scene.

Revising the Storyboard

If you do a good job creating a storyboard, you'll have an easy time filming your video. Remember, however, that you might need to revise your storyboard when you get into the editing stage. Be thinking about special effects, music, and titles, which you won't add yet but will need in the editing phase.

1 Sketch the Key Scenes

A storyboard is a cartoon you draw that describes, scene by scene or frame by frame, what happens in your movie. Draw all the events, depicting the video from key camera angles you intend to shoot. You can use a storyboard as a road map to filming the video.

2 Add Narrative

Under each frame, describe what is happening, who is in the scene, and what everyone is saying. You can also describe the mood or any other key elements.

Close up of Susan.

Zoom out as Peter enters scene and they look at each other.

3 Write the Script

At this stage, it's also important to write a script that identifies what everyone is going to say. The script will help identify any weaknesses in the storyboard and also flesh out the video you are about to film.

Close up of Susan.

Zoom out as Peter enters scene and they look at each other.

Script: Susan: "Where's the money?"

Peter: "I couldn't get it away from Tony."

4 Build the Props List

The last thing you need to do is detail any costumes, props, and other essential items you must have available. Place this information under each frame of the storyboard where appropriate.

Close up of Susan.

Zoom out as Peter enters scene and they look at each other.

Script: Susan: "Where's the money?"

Peter: "I couldn't get it away from Tony."

Props: Peter has gun

End

How to Handle DV Tapes

Although I refer to them as DV camcorders, they're really **MiniDV**, a smaller version of the DV standard. That's actually great because the MiniDV tapes that these camcorders use are tiny— about the size of a pair of AA batteries. Handle them carefully, and they'll take great movies.

The compact size of the cassette means that it is easy to carry.

Tapes come in a variety of lengths.

The new MiniDV cassettes are about the size of a couple of AA batteries.

Fixing Broken Tapes

It's possible for tapes to break, especially if they are used over and over again. Many camera and video shops will fix broken tapes for a small fee, usually under $15. If the break occurs in the middle of the tape, you'll lose a few seconds of video; if the tape breaks in the leader, it's possible that no data will be lost at all.

1 Open the Camera

DV camcorders must be turned on before you can load and eject tapes. Turn your camera on and then press and release the **Eject** button. The camera will open, exposing the loading mechanism.

2 Insert the Tape

Insert the tape cassette so that its spindles face down into the camera's mechanism and the tape faces the read/write heads at the front of the camera. It's not possible to put the tape in backward or upside down, so if you encounter resistance, check the cassette's orientation.

3 Close the Camera

Now you must close the camera—*but be careful!* You can damage the camera by applying pressure to the wrong part. You should press down to lock the cassette in place, taking note of any labels on the camera to indicate where to press.

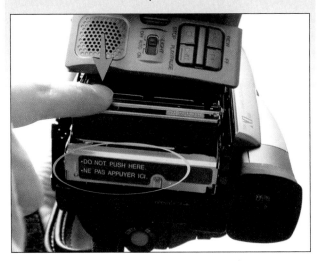

4 Tension the Tape

The first time you use a tape, it's a good idea to fast-forward to the end, and then rewind the tape back to the beginning. This action applies a uniform level of tension across all parts of the tape.

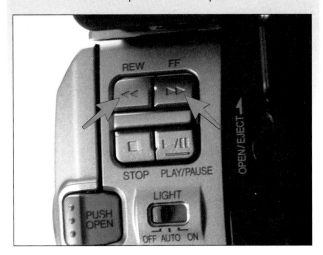

End

How to Zoom Effectively

The zoom feature on your camcorder is a valuable tool for composing your shots and capturing just the right elements in each scene. Specific *focal lengths* also give your movies a certain look. Telephoto shots, for instance, compress the foreground and background while keeping only the subject in sharp focus; more moderate lens magnifications are good for keeping everything in the image in focus at the same time.

High zoom magnification blurs the background.

Subject is in sharp focus.

Zooming eliminates background clutter.

Digital Zoom Warning

People often buy a particular camcorder because it offers a massive zoom—something along the lines of 200X or 300X. In reality, that number refers to a *digital zoom*, not an *optical zoom*. Optical zooms use the camera's optics to enlarge the image. But digital zooms use electronic trickery to increase the magnification, and the results are often noisy, grainy, and ugly. Avoid using the digital zoom very often—try to stick within the limits of the camera's optical zoom.

1 Use the Zoom Button

Your camera should have a lever or dial for controlling the zoom. Press it one way to zoom toward wide angle, and in the other direction for telephoto. Note that many cameras use one dial or lever to do several things, such as change volume and zoom the lens (as the VOL dial in this example does).

2 Enable Digital Zooming

Your camera probably has a digital zoom mode that extends your ability to zoom well past the optical zoom of the camera. You probably have to refer to your manual and enter the camera's menu system to turn on this zoom feature, which can enable you to magnify the view up to as much as 300X. (Optical zooms generally max out at about 12X.)

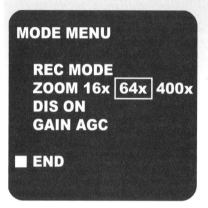

3 Zoom Slowly

Zooming takes patience and restraint to do well. Generally, you should zoom slowly (abrupt changes in zoom look bad on film) and zoom only once or twice in a scene. Watch television to see how professionals zoom: They do not overuse this technique. In fact, try to zoom between shots so that the viewer doesn't see the zoom happen.

4 Focus Manually

If you use the digital zoom mode and perform some extreme magnifications (such as 64X or more), the camcorder might have a hard time focusing automatically. If that's the case, you can disable your camera's auto-focus mode to focus manually, usually by turning a dial or ring. Refer to your camera manual for how to do that.

End

How to Use Motion Blur

It's hard to get the impression of speed in video—even if you're filming something that's going 100 miles per hour, it can look relatively stationary on a small television screen. That's why some people like

motion blur, which is the effect of tracking a speeding object and thus blurring the background because of the motion. Here's how to do it.

Slow shutter speed blurs background.

It takes practice to follow the moving subject accurately.

Track the subject to keep it sharp.

Zoom out far enough to see lots of background.

Motion Blur Tips

Motion blur is a powerful tool for conveying the sense of motion. Keep these tips in mind:

- Motion should be across your field of view, not from front to back. Because you want to blur the background, the camera must pan quickly.

- Slow shutter speeds help blur the background, but you'll need a steady hand to keep the subject in the same location in the viewfinder throughout the shot.

- Mounting the camcorder on a tripod and swiveling the head can help create a smooth, professional shot.

1 Set a Slow Shutter Speed

You can get decent motion blur even with your camera set on full automatic, but the slower your shutter speed is set, the better your results will be. I suggest that you set your camera's shutter to manual mode and try 1/30 or 1/60 second.

```
SHUTTER MENU
     1/60    SHUTTER
     1/100   SHUTTER
     1/250   SHUTTER
     1/500   SHUTTER
SEL ▶  OFF
```

2 Set the Focus Manually

In certain situations, you might not be able to keep the moving subject in the middle of the frame where the auto-focus sensors are located. If that's the case, set the focus to manual and dial in the focus to where the moving subject will be when you start shooting.

Prefocus to this distance before filming or use autofocus

3 Zoom Out

Before the shot begins, make sure that you're not zoomed in too far. If you can't see enough of the background, the effect of the motion blur will be lost.

4 Pan and Film

Time to get the shot. Start recording and pan with the moving object. Ideally, it will move from left to right (or right to left) across your field of view. Just turn with the moving object to keep it in the frame throughout the shot.

Pan

End

How to Light the Scene

Properly exposing video is a bit different than setting the exposure on a still camera, but the principles are the same. You can keep your camera in auto mode all the time, or you can take control and get better results with manual overrides. Every camcorder is different; to learn how to access your camera's manual exposure mode, refer to the documentation that came with the camcorder.

Lower lighting level reduces depth of focus, blurring background.

Filming in the shade reduces harsh light.

Reflector adds light to face.

Exposure Explained

The camera exposes the scene by balancing the *shutter speed* (the amount of time each frame of film is exposed to light) with the *aperture setting* (the size of the opening that lets light through the lens). The bigger the aperture's f/stop—expressed as f/2, f/5.6, or f/22, for instance—the smaller the aperture opening.

Lighting Options

You can buy a large, collapsible reflector from any camera store to put additional light on your subject. Reflectors fold up small enough to fit in a camera bag but unfurl quickly to put indirect light on your subject. If you can, consider multiple light sources. A *key light* is the main light in the room and often works best when combined with a *fill light* that is reflected off another surface to soften the effect. A *backlight* is reflected off the background to add a sense of distance between the subject and the background.

1 Stay in the Shade

When you shoot outdoors, direct sunlight can overwhelm your camcorder and create unflattering lighting or harsh shadows on your subject. Film in a shaded area whenever possible, and keep the sun to your left or right, never directly in front or behind you.

2 Go Manual When Moving

When you move from indoors to outdoors within a scene, the sudden change in lighting conditions can radically underexpose or overexpose the subject for a few seconds while the camera adjusts. To avoid that problem, set the exposure manually and leave it there through the scene transition. The background is less important than the subject is!

3 Use a Reflector

A reflector is especially useful outdoors, where you can position someone who is holding it off to the side of your subject. This kind of light is more flattering to people than harsh, direct sunlight.

4 Use Multiple Lights

When filming indoors, you have a lot more control over the lighting. If you're in a really controlled situation, such as shooting a talking head or an interview, I recommend that you use two or three lights to illuminate your subject.

End

How to Control Depth of Focus

Beginning videographers rarely think about the subtleties of filmmaking, but it's the little things that can really make your projects look professional and have that extra punch. One such aspect is *depth of* *field*, which determines how much of the scene is in sharp focus. Creative use of depth of field can have a powerful, dramatic role in your films.

A blurred background makes the subject stand out.

This effect is achieved with a telephoto zoom or an open aperture.

Depth of Field Explained

Depth of field—the amount of the scene that remains in focus in front and in back of the focused subject—depends on both the amount of zoom and the aperture setting of the camera. Use depth of field to isolate the subject from the foreground and background or to keep the entire scene in focus. Unlike the process with a 35 mm SLR camera, you don't have to do anything special to "check" the depth of field you are filming; what you see through the viewfinder is what you get on film.

1 Zoom In: Less Depth

An easy way to reduce depth of field to isolate your subject is to work at the telephoto end of the optical zoom on your camera. However, note that zooming into the digital zoom ratios on your camera has no effect on depth of field.

2 Zoom Out: More Depth

You achieve the most depth of field by zooming out to the camera's most wide-angle setting. At this setting, virtually all of the scene should be in sharp focus.

3 Open Aperture: Less Depth

If you can switch to the camcorder's manual mode, opening the aperture to admit more light also has the effect of reducing depth of field. In this example, note that although the camera lens is zoomed out to capture both children, the wide-open aperture setting narrows depth of field so that the focus is only on the child in front.

4 Close Aperture: More Depth

In manual exposure mode, if you shut down the aperture to smaller values, you reduce the light entering the lens and simultaneously increase depth of field, making more of the scene in focus. In this example, note that the lens is zoomed out about the same as it was for the children in the preceding step, but the smaller aperture setting forces a deeper field of focus.

End

How to White-Balance Your Scene

Camcorders have to be tuned to the particular color of light you are filming in; otherwise, colors (such as flesh tones) look wrong. When your camcorder knows what color white is, all the other colors come out accurately as well. This adjustment is usually done automatically, but you can get better results by manually white-balancing your camcorder—especially indoors, in low-light situations, when using a camera light, or with unusually tinted overhead lights.

Switch to automatic white balance or recalibrate when conditions change.

Have your subject or an assistant hold a paper near the subject's face, where color accuracy is most important.

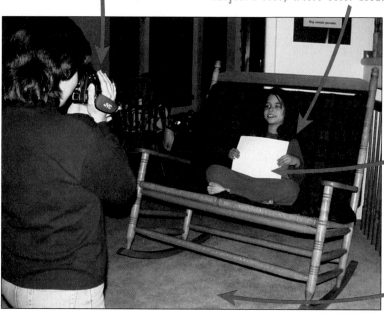

Use plain white paper to perform a manual white balance.

Experiment with white balance to see what kinds of locations require manual settings.

Why Balance Your Whites?

Different light sources (such as light provided by sunrise, midday sun, candlelight, and fluorescent bulbs) have different color temperatures, and this affects the way your camera displays color. An improperly balanced scene will appear reddish or bluish, depending on the color temperature. For the most accurate video, balance your whites often, and don't trust the automatic controls unless you have to.

Remember to reset your white balance whenever conditions change. If you use manual white balance settings from indoors when you film outdoors, you'll get very unusual results.

1 Enter the Menu

The exact procedure for balancing whites manually depends on the kind of camera you have, but most white balancing procedures are similar. Start by entering the White Balance menu and selecting manual mode.

W. BALANCE   MANUAL

■ END

2 Focus on White Paper

Have someone hold a piece of bright white paper in front of the camera. Position yourself so that the paper fills the frame and is in focus. Also, be sure that the paper is bathed in the light that you plan to shoot your subjects in so that you balance the camera properly.

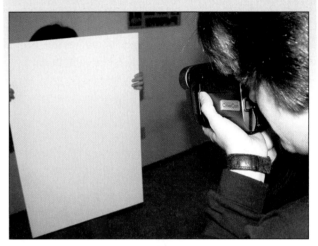

3 Set the Balance

Refer to your camera's documentation to learn how to set the white balance. (The JVC camera in this example uses the Menu dial to lock in the white balance.) Then select the appropriate control on the camera to "memorize" the color value of the paper. This sets the white balance for the current lighting conditions.

4 Exit the Menu

Finish the process by exiting the white balance menu. The camera is now set for filming. Remember that when you're done filming this scene, you should either set the camera back to automatic white balance or recalibrate the manual white balance for the next set of lighting conditions.

FOCUS   AUTO
EXPOSURE   AUTO
W. BALANCE   AUTO
FADER   OFF

■ END

End

How to Take Low-Light Movies

Camcorders are rated by their *lux value*, which indicates how low the light can be before the camera can't record an image. Lux values are subjective and are not standard, but typically a 2-lux camera can work in candlelight. That's not bad, but you need to know how to get the most out of low-light situations.

Manual white balance corrects the color of the scene (using the automatic white balance, these flames would be orange).

Camera light fills in the subject's face.

Use overhead lights if available.

Video is grainy in low-light situations.

Low-Light Pitfalls

Although you can film in low-light situations with most camcorders, keep these tips in mind for best results:

- Auto-focus systems fail in low light. You might need to resort to manual focusing if you're filming by candlelight.

- The quality of light varies dramatically in a dark room. When you set the white balance, put the white card exactly where you plan to film.

- The quality of video recorded in low light will be dramatically lower than the quality of video recorded in daylight.

1 Set White Balance

Low-light situations are almost certainly outside the camera's preset white balance values. Whenever filming in these situations, the first thing you should do is set the camera's white balance. If the lighting changes during the shoot, reset the white balance as often as necessary.

2 Use Lights

Camera lights are often harsh and unforgiving, but they are essential if you're trying to film in very low-light conditions. Your camera might have a built-in light you can turn on, or you can purchase a clip-on camera light.

3 Avoid Digital Zoom

In low-light situations, the image will probably be grainy—this is digital noise that occurs when there isn't enough light to make a good shot. Digital zooming introduces noise of its own, so avoid that feature when you film in the dark.

Here is 64X digital zoom in ordinary lighting.

4 Use Night Vision

In near or absolute darkness, you might be able to use another feature: infrared recording. This feature is found in Sony Handycams, where it goes by the name **NightShot**. NightShot works only up to about 10 feet away from the camera and creates a greenish monochrome image similar to what you would see through night-vision goggles.

End

How to Reduce Camera Shake

Many digital cameras come with a feature known as *digital image stabilization*. Image stabilization can be used to reduce the apparent jitter or shakiness in a scene, especially when you're using the zoom. There are other ways to stabilize your image, too.

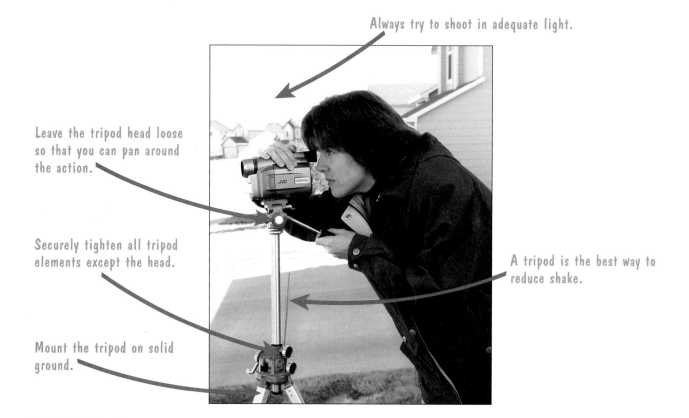

Always try to shoot in adequate light.

Leave the tripod head loose so that you can pan around the action.

Securely tighten all tripod elements except the head.

Mount the tripod on solid ground.

A tripod is the best way to reduce shake.

When Not to Stabilize

Electronic stabilization tries to mimic the SteadiCam, a device used by pros to reduce vibration when filming with a moving camera. Unfortunately, digital artifacts can be obvious when using this feature. Avoid it when filming in low light, when using the digital zoom, or when shooting scenes with lots of obvious stripes (such as Venetian blinds). All these situations increase the potential for digital noise on film if your camera is set to use its electronic stabilization feature.

1 Enable the Stabilization Mode

When you're in a situation where you want to minimize the jitters that come from camera shake, enable your camera's digital image stabilization mode. You can find it in the camera's menu; refer to the manual for details on where to find it.

2 Move Slowly

Regardless of whether you're using electronic stabilization, try to move the camera slowly and steadily. Don't jerk the camera around. Note that fast zooming can induce motion sickness in your audience. Zoom slowly and keep any zooming you do to a minimum.

3 Use a Tripod

The best way to stabilize a scene is by mounting your camcorder on a tripod. Leave the swivel head loose so that you can move the camera from side to side and up and down while you film.

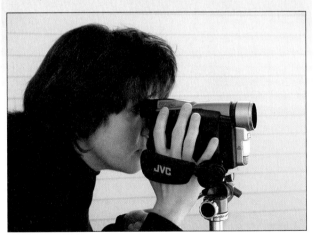

4 Get Support from a Doorway

If you can't use a tripod, try leaning your body against something solid (such as a doorway, a fence, or a post) for support. This trick really works.

End

How to Film with a Blue Screen

Special effects in movies are often done with a *blue screen.* By filming the action in front of a specially colored backdrop, another video layer can later replace the background. You can do the same thing with your camcorder—although it takes practice and careful planning. Keep in kind that the blue screen does not have to be a backdrop. In this task, I intentionally have my subject hold a blue-screen matte so that you can see the effect of adding a layer of video at some random location in the scene.

Keep the blue screen lit evenly for best results.

Keep the color tolerance low enough so that you don't spill video into the rest of your scene.

Foreground video.

Background video.

Use a unique color for your "blue screen."

Your First Blue Screen

Special effects such as blue screens are the most fun and rewarding parts of experimenting with a camcorder. But good blue-screen mattes are hard to get. To get your feet wet, try filming one person in front of a solid wall. You might also try putting a piece of brightly colored poster paper on the wall to get an evening news "weather map" effect. If you have success with these videos, step up to making moving action against a colored backdrop.

1 Find a Backdrop

Your backdrop doesn't have to be blue, but it should be a very different color than anything else in the scene. You needn't fill the whole background with the backdrop; a small square can serve as a weather map or window.

2 Test It First

Before you bank on the backdrop working, test it first. Film the backdrop with your camcorder and then import the clip into VideoWave or Premiere to see whether you can make your particular blue screen work (see Part 4, Task 15, "How to Create Special Effects with a Blue Screen," for details).

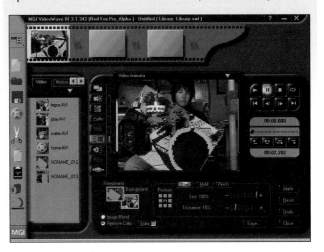

3 Light It Carefully

The backdrop should be lit evenly, with no obvious shadows or highlights. It might take more than one backlight or reflector to illuminate the backdrop properly. Make sure that any people in front of the backdrop don't cast shadows on the material.

4 Edit

After you have your video on tape, you'll need to use the **Chroma key** transparency filter in either VideoWave or Premiere to let another layer of video "see through" the backdrop; see Part 4, Task 10, "How to Superimpose Video," for details.

End

How to Add In-the-Lens Transitions

Transitions are graphical segues that signal the end of one scene and the start of the next. A transition can be as simple as a fade-out or as complex as seeing one clip fly off-screen as another clip enters the picture. Your camcorder probably has the capability to perform some simple transitions, eliminating the need to create them on the PC. In these steps, you learn how to create a transition directly in the camcorder, without using the PC.

Leading edge of wipe.

Second scene.

First scene.

Camera stores the wipe on tape.

The PC Does It Better

If you don't want to edit your movie on a PC, adding transitions between scenes in the camera may be okay. But you can get snazzier results with editing software such as VideoWave or Premiere. If you do want to edit your video on a PC, don't use in-camera fades and wipes. If you use fades and wipes, you make it harder to separate scenes for editing because they're "glued together" on tape with a transition.

1 Enable Fades or Wipes

Refer to your camcorder's manual and find the menu setting for the automatic transitions, usually called a **fade**, **wipe**, or **dissolve**. You should see a short menu of possible options to choose from.

```
FOCUS        AUTO
EXPOSURE     AUTO
W. BALANCE   AUTO
FADER       [ ON ]


■ END
```

2 Select the Transition

Pick the transition you'd like to use. A *fade* "fades" from black or white; a *wipe* or a *slide* physically moves the new video into the frame while displacing the old video. A *dissolve* fades from one video to the next. For more complex transitions, you'll have to move your video to the PC.

```
FADER
         WIPE-SLIDE
         DISSOLVE
         RANDOM
SEL ▶    OFF
         FADER-WHITE
         FADER-BLACK
```

3 Record Your Scene

The transition effect happens automatically when you press the **Record** button to start and stop recording. When you are done with the effect, remember to turn the transition feature off in the camera's menu.

4 Don't Turn Off the Camera

If you turn off your camcorder after filming a scene, the ending position will be lost and the camera can't use a transition to ease into the next scene you film.

End

Task

PART 3

Preparing Your PC for Video

Your computer is a key ingredient in your digital video-editing suite. It must be fast enough, with just the right hardware to process video without dropping frames or garbling audio. A few years ago, that was a tall order, but today almost any Pentium II or faster PC is ready to rock.

You can never have too much PC, but your computer should be at least a Pentium II with 128MB of RAM, a 10GB hard drive, and a video capture card. The video capture card—called IEEE1394 or FireWire—connects the PC to your digital camcorder and lets you copy the video from the tape to your hard drive. After the video is on the computer, you can edit your movie and then send it back to tape (through the FireWire card, of course) so that you can give copies of your masterpiece to friends, family, co-workers, and so on. In this part of the book, I'll talk about how to make sure that your computer is ready to edit. ●

How to Install More Memory

Make no mistake: Video editing takes a lot of memory. Your video-editing program will need to load a lot of data into memory at once, and if you don't have enough RAM, what doesn't fit in RAM will be temporarily stored on the hard disk, slowing down your PC and making your video appear jerky and unprofessional. For best results, you should have at least 128MB of RAM. Installing additional memory is easy—the hardest part is getting the case of your computer open.

128MB of RAM is the least you should have to edit video.

Don't use disk compression; get a bigger hard disk.

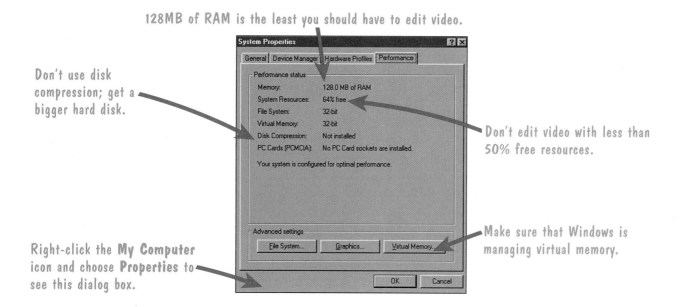

Don't edit video with less than 50% free resources.

Make sure that Windows is managing virtual memory.

Right-click the **My Computer** icon and choose **Properties** to see this dialog box.

Troubleshooting Memory

Adding memory is one of the easiest things you can do to the inside of the PC. You can run into trouble, however. Check these items:

- Is it the right kind of memory? You usually can't mix memory modules on a motherboard, even if there are sockets for both DIMMs and SIMMs. Check your computer manual to see which kind you need.

- Will the new memory work by itself? If your PC has a problem with the new memory, remove the old stuff and try the new modules by themselves.

- Will the new memory work in another PC? The final test for memory that doesn't seem to work is to see whether it'll work in another PC. If not, it's defective.

1 Get the Right Memory

Check your computer's manual or open your PC to see what's inside. Memory comes in two main flavors: 72-pin EDO RAM (which comes on a chip called a SIMM) and 168-pin SDRAM (which comes on a DIMM). SDRAM DIMMs are the most common, and you can get a 64MB or 128MB DIMM module fairly inexpensively, either from a local computer store or the Internet.

2 Locate the Memory Slot

Open your PC's case, make sure that you're electrically grounded (touch a grounded metal surface), and locate an empty memory socket. If you're dealing with old-style SIMMs, you'll need to install memory in pairs. DIMMs can be installed singly. Here you see two DIMM slots, ready for new memory chips.

3 Insert Your RAM

Depending on the kind of socket on your motherboard, there are two ways to insert the memory. One method: Insert the module in the socket at a 45-degree angle and then roll the module by pushing on its top until it clicks into place, held securely by the metal clips at each end. The second method (as seen here): Press the module down firmly until the end clips snap up to lock the module in place.

4 Test Your PC

Put the cover back on your PC and turn it on. You should see the new memory displayed when the PC runs through its startup test. If your computer doesn't recognize the correct amount of memory, the memory was mismarked at the store, a module is bad, or your computer simply doesn't support that much memory. After starting Windows, right-click **My Computer** and choose **Properties**.

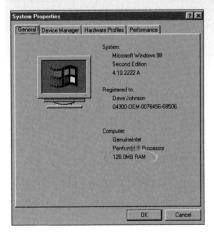

End

How to Install a New Hard Drive

TASK 2

Many new computers come with huge hard drives that are more than sufficient for working with video files. If you have an older PC, however, consider installing a big hard drive before going any further with video editing. Video files are huge—digital video files take up about 250MB per minute of recorded video. You should have a dedicated hard drive that is no less than 10GB in size if you want to make a 30-minute film.

If you can afford it, dedicate one hard drive just for video.

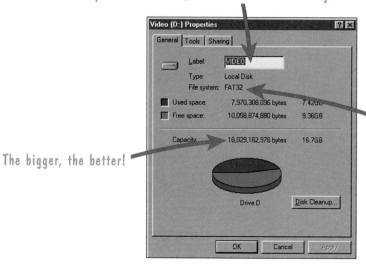

Make sure that the drive is formatted with the FAT32 filing system.

The bigger, the better!

Ultimate Video with Ultra ATA/66

If you're installing a new hard drive anyway, you should make sure that it's Ultra ATA/66-compatible. This is the fastest kind of consumer hard drive available, and it will ensure that you won't have any stutters or jitters in your video because of the drive. Check to see whether your motherboard has an Ultra ATA/66 controller onboard. If not, install such a controller in an empty PCI slot in your PC (Promise, at http://www.promise.com, makes an excellent Ultra ATA/66 controller card) and connect the drive to the controller instead of to the motherboard.

1 Set the Jumpers

The trickiest part of installing a hard disk is setting the jumpers correctly. A **master** drive has an IDE cable all to itself or is the first drive in a line. A **slave** drive is the second drive on an IDE cable, after the master. Check the manual that came with the drive to set the jumpers appropriately for both the old and new drives.

The hard drive's Master/Slave jumper.

2 Install the Rails

Find the drive bay into which you plan to install the drive. If you are installing a slave drive, you must position it close enough to the master drive that the IDE cable will reach. If the drive requires special rails to fit in the bay, install them now and then slide the drive into place.

Screwing the rails onto the side of the hard drive.

3 Connect the Cables

Connect both the IDE cable and the power cable to the drive. If you've run out of free power cords inside the PC, most computer shops sell Y-shaped splitters. If you're trying to take full advantage of an Ultra ATA/66 drive and an ATA/66 controller, you must use a special IDE cable, which usually has a unique blue marker on it.

IDE cable.   Power cable.

4 Format the Drive

With your drive securely screwed in and connected, turn on your PC. Your BIOS should recognize the drive automatically; if not, enter the BIOS setup program (usually by pressing **F1** or **Delete** at startup) and configure the BIOS. Then use the software that came with the drive to format your new drive for use. After formatting, the drive should appear in the **My Computer** folder.

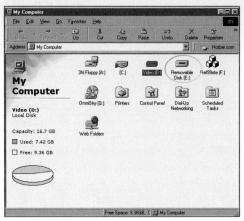

End

How to Install a Video Capture Card

If you were lucky enough to buy a video-ready multimedia PC, your computer might already be poised to begin importing video clips from a camcorder. If not, you'll have to install a video capture card. I recommend that you get a FireWire card (also called an IEEE1394 card) to go with a DV camcorder. An analog video capture card will work too, but at a lower overall video resolution. Regardless of the kind of card you choose, it takes only a screwdriver and a few minutes to install it.

The "choke" is closest to the PC.

FireWire card installed in a PCI slot.

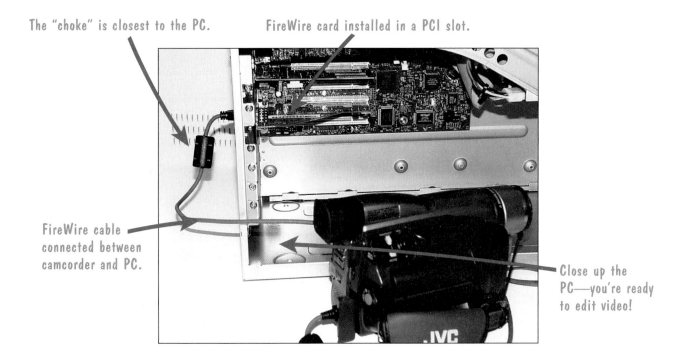

FireWire cable connected between camcorder and PC.

Close up the PC—you're ready to edit video!

Choosing a Video Card

A video capture card is essential to the video editing process because the card is what lets you import video from your camcorder to the PC. Most capture devices are internal models that slip into a PCI slot, but there are also USB models around that are completely external—a real convenience. Remember, though, that video capture hardware is finicky. Make sure that your capture card is certified to work with the software you plan to use (such as VideoWave or Premiere) before you buy and install it. Adobe, for instance, lists compatible FireWire cards at **www.adobe.com/premiere**.

1 Open Your PC

Start by opening your PC, usually by removing several screws from the back. Remember to ground yourself (touch some other grounded metal object) before you touch anything inside the computer.

2 Slip the Card in Place

Find an empty PCI slot in the computer and unscrew the plate from the back of the computer (retain the screw). Take the card out of its anti-static bag and press it into the empty slot. It might help to rock the card back and forth to get it in place. Be firm, but don't press so hard that the card bends and cracks. Use the plate screw to screw the card in place.

Back plate removed.

3 Attach the Cables

If you're installing a FireWire card, all you have to do is attach a single FireWire cable to the card (the other end plugs into your DV camcorder). If you've installed a traditional analog capture card, you'll have to plug in a video cable and audio cables as well.

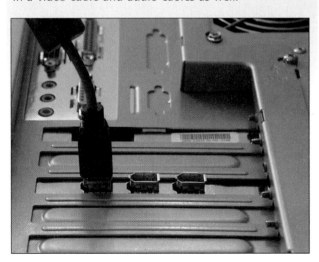

4 Install the Software

Follow the directions that came with the card to install the software. There will be a driver that tells your PC about the card, as well as video editing software. You can use that editing software or another package, such as VideoWave or Premiere, as long as the card and the software are compatible. After the driver is installed, you'll see the capture card in your PC's **System Properties** dialog box.

End

How to Optimize Your Hard Drive

TASK *4*

Hard drives are great at making data files fit in small places. A large file is automatically split into a lot of little chunks on a well-used hard drive, for instance, and Windows usually doesn't care. But video files work best when they're stored in one big piece; otherwise, your video quality might suffer. The solution? Before every video production session, you should optimize your hard drive. This arranges files on the drive so that you have a large empty space in which you can store your video file in a single chunk.

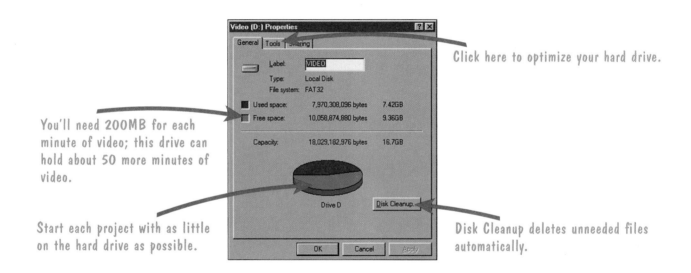

Click here to optimize your hard drive.

You'll need 200MB for each minute of video; this drive can hold about 50 more minutes of video.

Start each project with as little on the hard drive as possible.

Disk Cleanup deletes unneeded files automatically.

Take Care of Your Hard Drive

A well-tuned hard drive is important to maintaining good video quality. Always shut down your PC using the **Start menu** (choose **Start, Shut Down**) to avoid corrupting files, and delete data and applications that you don't need to keep free space available.

1 Delete Unneeded Files

When you're ready to create a video, the first thing you should do is display the contents of the hard drive you use to store your video files and delete any files—especially big ones—that you no longer need. Remember to empty the trash when you're done. Another way to do this: run the **Disk Cleanup** wizard on the **General** tab in the hard drive's **Properties** dialog box.

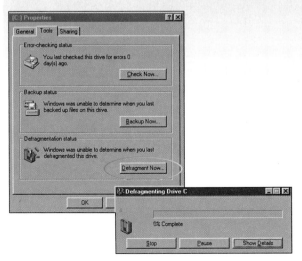

Right-click

2 Scan Your Disk

After you've pruned your drive, check for errors. Double-click the **My Computer** icon on the desktop to see the drives, and then right-click the drive you use for video. Choose **Properties** from the context menu and click the **Tools** tab of the **Properties** dialog box that opens. In the **Error-checking status** section, click **Check Now**. The **Scan Disk** dialog box opens. Make sure that the drive you use to store video is selected and click **Start** to begin.

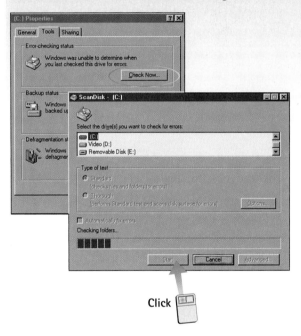

Click

3 Defragment the Drive

After the drive has been checked for errors and repaired as necessary, you should *defragment* the drive. (That is, arrange the data to leave large contiguous sections of the drive available for video files.) On the **Tools** tab of the drive's **Properties** dialog box, click **Defragment Now**. The defragment process might take a while—hours, even—to complete.

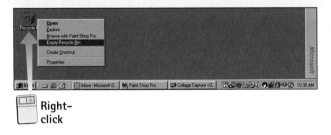

4 Reboot Your PC

After you're done optimizing your hard drive, reboot the PC using the **Start**, **Shut Down** menu option. Select the **Restart** option and click **OK** to reboot.

Click

End

How to Capture Video

You're about ready to start editing video! The first step to working with video on the PC is downloading it to the computer from your camcorder (or VCR).

After the files are stored on your PC, you can edit them in your video editor—which is the subject of the rest of this book.

Add other clips on your hard drive to the library.

Here is a library of captured clips you can use in your video.

Enter Capture mode.

Start and stop capturing video.

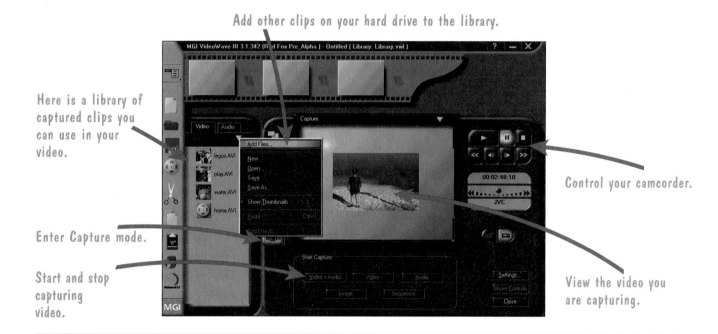

Control your camcorder.

View the video you are capturing.

Capture Card Compatibility

In many cases, getting video into your PC is the single most complex and heart-wrenching step in the editing process. If you can complete this step without a problem, you're halfway home. But if your video editing software won't capture video, that's probably because the software doesn't work with the capture card you have installed (a common problem), or you need a new capture card driver. The easiest solution: Contact the video editor vendor directly (MGI for VideoWave, or Adobe for Premiere) and ask the representative about your capture card. The rep should tell you whether the card should work or whether you need an updated driver (as well as where to get it). Your first stop to troubleshoot capture problems should be the Web. Try **www.adobe.com** for Premiere and **www.mgisoft.com** for VideoWave.

1 Connect Your Cables V

Before you start the video capture software on the PC, make sure that the FireWire or audio/video cables are connected from the capture card in the PC to the camcorder or VCR. Turn on your camcorder or VCR and set it to **Play** mode (instead of **Record**). If necessary, put it in **Pause** mode until you're ready to capture.

2 Set Capture Mode V

If you are capturing video with VideoWave, start the program and click the **Capture** icon. VideoWave will switch to Capture mode and display video from the camcorder onscreen. It won't actually start copying the video onto your hard drive until you tell it to, though.

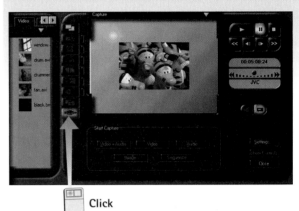

Click

3 Choose Your Camcorder V

If this is the first time you're capturing video in VideoWave, you might have to select your camcorder in the program settings. (This is especially true when you have another kind of camera installed on the PC, such as a Webcam.) Click the **Settings** button and choose the appropriate device from the **Capture Device** list menu; then click **OK**.

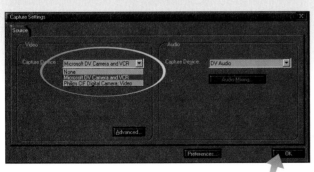

Click

4 Start Capturing V

If you want to capture video that already exists on the camcorder's videotape, click the **VTR** mode button. Click the **Camera** button to record "live" video—that is, what the camcorder is currently seeing through its lens. When you are ready to capture, use the VCR-style controls on the VideoWave screen to control the camcorder. Click the **Video+Audio** button to start recording; click the **Stop** button to end the capture.

Control the camcorder playback.

Click to start and stop capturing.

Click **VTR** to capture from tape; click **Camera** to capture live video.

continues

1 Set Capture Mode **P**

If you're using Premiere, setting the capture device is a bit more involved. After the camcorder is turned on, start Premiere and choose **Settings, Capture** from the menu. The **Project Settings** dialog box opens.

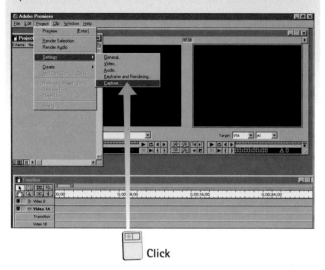

Click

2 Open the VfW Settings **P**

Click the **VfW Settings** button to open the **Video for Windows Capture Options** dialog box.

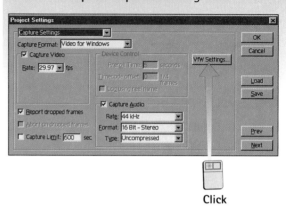

Click

3 Open the Video Input Dialog Box **P**

Click the **Video Input** button to open the **Video Source** dialog box.

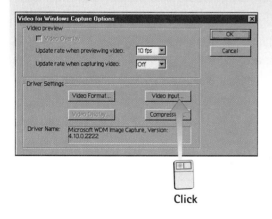

Click

4 Choose Your Camera **P**

Finally, choose your camcorder from the **Select a Video Device** drop-down list. Click **OK** to close all the open dialog boxes; you're now ready to capture.

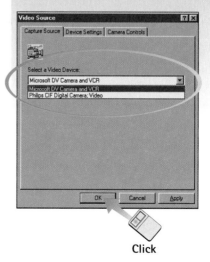

Click

5 Open the Capture Window **P**

Choose **File, Capture, Video Capture** from the menu. The **Movie Capture** window should appear. Note that some capture cards don't work with Premiere; if you have one of those cards, you'll have to capture your video with the software that came with the card and import it into Premiere later.

6 Capture Your Video **P**

Start rolling the videotape in your camcorder and then click the **Record** button to capture your clip. When you're done recording video to the computer's hard drive, press the **Escape** key to stop capturing. The clip appears in a new window.

Click

7 Drag the Clip **P**

If you want to use this clip in your video, position the mouse pointer in the middle of the clip window, click and hold the mouse button, and then drag the clip into the **Project** window. You'll have to save the file before it can be added to your project.

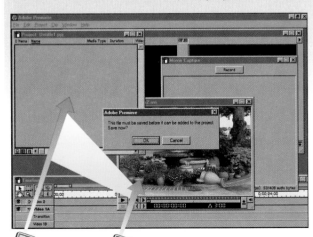

Drop   Drag

8 Close the Clip Window **P**

With the clip safely stored on your hard drive and appearing in the **Project** window, close the **Clip** window by clicking the close box in the window's title bar.

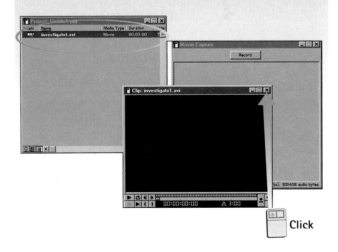

Click

End

Task

PART 4

Editing Your Movie

We've finally reached the fun part of the process. With the video *clips*—the scenes of your movie—stored on your PC's hard drive, it's time to mold them into a film. The tasks in this part of the book cover all the basics—generating the overall structure of your film, adding transitions, editing the scenes, and even creating special effects.

Later in the book, you'll learn how to incorporate titles and sound into the movie as well. When all the basics are in place, you'll finish the process by *producing* your movie. That final step takes all the separate video clips and renders them into a single, high-quality movie that can be played back on videotape, the Web, or CD-ROM. As you work your way through the tasks in this part, keep in mind that your movie, at this stage, is still "unassembled"—you can get only a rough idea of the final product when you preview it.

From this point on in the book, we use MGI VideoWave and Adobe Premiere (both are found on the CD-ROM at the back of the book) to create your movies. If you're new to video editing, try VideoWave. It has a lot of features, yet it's extremely easy to use. When you want to try more advanced tricks and discover that VideoWave can't quite get you there, try Premiere. I hand-picked both of these programs for the book because I believe they represent the best video editors on the market. You can't go wrong with either of them.

For now, let's get started laying out your movie. ●

How to Prepare the Editor

When you first start your video editor, it is not necessarily ready to start creating your masterpiece. In the case of VideoWave, for instance, the video clip library might be filled with sample clips and the Storyline might have unwanted bits of an old video in it. This task explains how you can start the creation of any new video project with a clean slate.

Blank Storyline.

Viewscreen.

Menu button.

New production.

VCR controls.

Library of video clips.

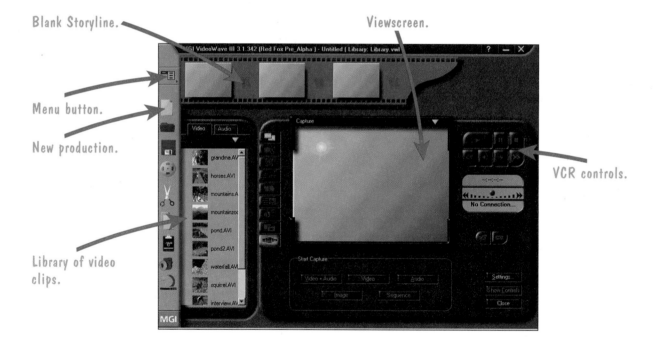

Make Sure That Your PC Is Ready

Before starting any video project, it's a good idea to run through the hard disk maintenance steps outlined in Part 3 of this book, "Using Your PC for Video." Specifically, try these important steps:

- Delete unwanted video clips before you begin. Video clips are huge and take up space you might need to render your video.

- Run ScanDisk to detect any errors on your hard drive.

- Defragment your hard drive to make sure that clips play fast, without jitters or hiccups.

1 Clear the Storyline

In VideoWave parlance, the *Storyline* is the set of panels that run across the top of the screen. Each panel holds one scene in your video. To clear the Storyline and make it ready for a new project, click the **New Production** icon in the toolbar.

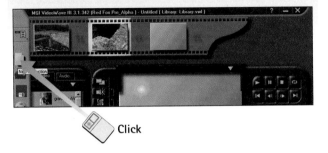

Click

2 Clear the Library

If the Library is full of clips that aren't a part of your video, you can clear them all out at once by clicking the list menu arrowhead and choosing **New**. To delete individual clips, click the clip you want to delete and press the **Delete** key; when prompted, decide whether you want to remove the clip from the hard disk entirely or just from the Library list.

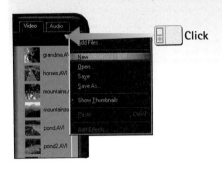

Click

3 Load Clips into the Library

Load all the video clips you want to use into the Library. To do that, click the list menu arrowhead and choose **Add Files**. In the **Open** dialog box that appears, locate the video files you captured on your hard drive (see Part 3, Task 5, "How to Capture Video," for more information) and click **Open** to make those files available in the Library.

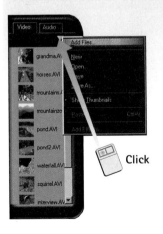

Click

1 Configure Your Project 🅿

Some video editors, such as Premiere, can create a broad variety of video projects. They work best when you configure the software for the kind of video you want to make right at the beginning. Start Premiere and click the **Load** button. Choose a preset, or template, that reflects the kind of video you want to make, such as DV. The presets you see in your own copy of Premiere might differ from those you see here, depending on the kind of capture card you have and the kinds of files it supplies to Premiere.

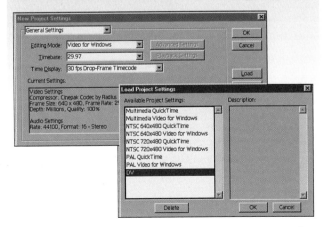

End

How to Populate the Storyline

The first step in any video project is to lay out the clips you plan to use in the video editor's timeline or storyboard. VideoWave uses a storyboard concept—the panels at the top of the screen represent sequential scenes in your video, which MGI calls a *Storyline*. Premiere is more traditional; it uses the concept of a timeline. In Premiere, you drag clips to the Timeline, where they appear stacked like a bar graph.

Storyline.

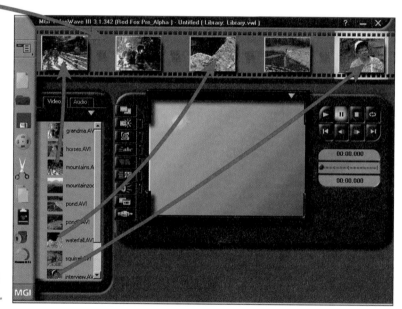

Drag and drop clips from the Library to positions on the Storyline to rough in the flow of the video.

Get Your Feet Wet with Templates

Hopefully you sketched your own storyboard for the video you want to create as outlined in Part 2 of this book. If you need more help, though, you'll be happy to know that VideoWave has a library of *storyboard templates* that can help you structure your video. If you need help organizing your film, open an appropriate storyboard from the **VideoWave\Media\Storyboard** folder. Each panel in the storyboard includes text that suggests a specific flow for your movie.

1 Preview Your Clips

Before you drag clips to the Storyline, you can preview them to make sure that you have the right clip in hand. Double-click a clip in the Library. The clip will appear in the Viewscreen. Click the VCR controls to play the clip and make sure that it's the one you want to use.

 Double-click

2 Drag and Drop

Now drag the clip from the Library and drop it on the Storyline. It'll appear in the first panel. To finish creating the rough draft of your video, continue dragging clips to the Storyline, dropping each to the right of the previous clip.

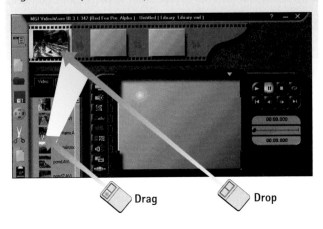

Drag   Drop

3 Preview from the Storyline

If you need to refresh your memory about what's in a Storyline clip, you can preview it from there as well. Just double-click any panel in the Storyline; the clip appears in the Viewscreen, where you can play it with the VCR controls.

 Double-click

1 Drag and Drop P

In Adobe Premiere, the idea is the same—double-click any clip in the **Project** window to preview it; drag it to the Timeline to add it to the video you are creating. Drag the clip to the **Video 1A** line; add subsequent clips to the **Video 1A** track by dropping them to the right of preceding clips.

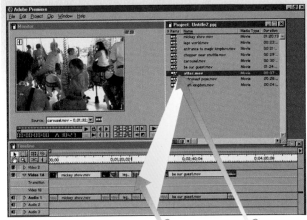

Drop   Drag

End

How to Rearrange Scenes

Even with a well-organized storyboard and the best of intentions, you're going to want to rearrange your video after the clips have been added to the Storyline. That's okay; it's easy to do. In fact, that's the magic of nonlinear editing: You can add, remove, and rearrange clips at will.

Drag from the Library between Storyline panels to insert a clip between existing clips.

Drag a clip to a new place on the Storyline to rearrange clips.

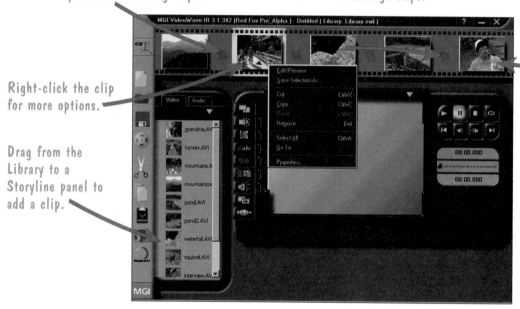

Right-click the clip for more options.

Drag from the Library to a Storyline panel to add a clip.

Select a panel and press **Delete** to remove the clip from the Storyline (but not from the Library).

Remember the Right Mouse Button

As with most Windows applications, VideoWave uses the right mouse button to simplify your work. Right-click any clip—either in the Library or the Storyline—and get a list of options such as copying, pasting, and deleting the video. Often, this is the most convenient way to work with a clip.

Rearranging Scenes in Premiere

If you're working in Premiere, editing clips is a snap. If you've added a few scenes to the Timeline, you can rearrange them just by dragging and dropping them from one position to another. Likewise, to delete a scene, just right-click the scene and press the **Delete** key.

1 Move Clips in the Storyline

If you decide that you want to move a clip to a different part of the movie, you can drag and drop it to the desired location. To move the clip in the Storyline, first click the clip to select it; click again, the second time holding down the mouse button. Then move the mouse, dragging the clip to the new location in the Storyline.

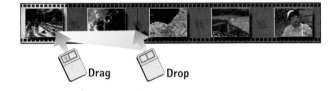

Drag   Drop

2 Delete a Scene

If you want to eliminate a clip from the Storyline, just click the clip to select it and press the **Delete** key on the keyboard. The clip is removed from the video but remains in the Library for you to use again. Alternatively, right-click the clip you want to delete and choose **Remove** from the shortcut menu.

Right-click

3 Insert a Scene

You already know how to add clips to the end of the Storyline. To add a clip to a location in the middle of the Storyline, just drag it from the Library to a position between two existing clips. When you release the mouse button, the clip will be inserted at that position.

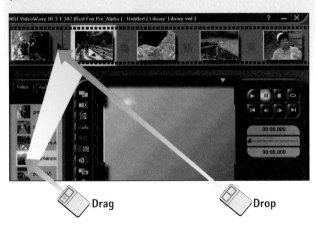

Drag   Drop

4 Duplicate a Scene

You might want to include the same scene in two parts of your video, especially if you edit them differently (as explained in Task 5, "How to Trim the Length of a Clip"). To copy a clip, right-click the original clip in the Storyline and choose **Copy** from the shortcut menu. Then right-click a blank panel in the Storyline and choose **Paste** from the shortcut menu.

Right-click

End

How to Save and Open Your Project

Because you probably can't create your entire video production and save it to tape or CD-ROM in a single sitting, at some point you'll have to save your work so that you can pick it up again later where you left off.

Choose **Storyline, Save** from the menu button.

Save your work often so that the most current version of your production is available.

Get Help from Preferences

Choose **Preferences** from VideoWave's menu button to access a few options that can make your life easier. In general, you probably want to **Save Library with Production** because that way you don't have to reload all your potential video clips every time you start the program. You might also want to **Open Last** Production on Start Up because that option saves you the trouble of loading the in-progress production every time you start the program. One last tip: Don't **Show Splash Screen on Startup** because it gets annoying after a while.

1 Save Your Work

Get in the habit of saving your work frequently because VideoWave won't do it for you. Choose **Storyline, Save As** from the menu button to give your production a name and save it. After the first time you save, you can choose **Storyline, Save** to quickly save your work. By default, your production file is given the extension **.sbd**.

Click

2 Open Your Production

When you start VideoWave and want to return to a saved production, choose **Storyline, Open** from the menu icon. The **Open** dialog box appears, from which you can select the project you want to work on.

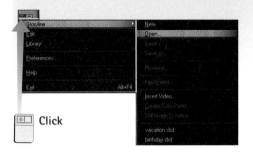

Click

1 Save Your Project P

In Premiere, the process of saving your work is very similar to that in VideoWave—but you can also set the program to automatically save your work at set intervals. To do that, choose **File, Preferences, AutoSave/Undo**. In the **Preferences** dialog box that opens, configure the program to save your work at any interval you desire.

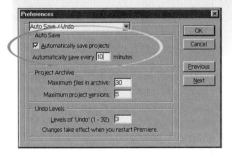

2 Open an AutoSaved Project P

If you want to open a project that has been automatically saved, you can't just choose **File, Open**. Instead, choose **File, Open** and look for the **Project-Archive** folder in the **Premiere** program folder. (A likely path is something like **C:\Program Files\Adobe\Premiere 5.1\Project-Archive**.)

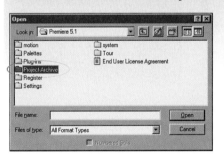

End

How to Trim the Length of a Clip

Just because a scene you shot on the camcorder is several minutes long doesn't mean it has to stay that way in the final production. In fact, video editors enable you to trim clips down to eliminate unwanted details, or to split a single clip into several scenes (as explained in the next task). In fact, clip editing is a powerful tool that lets you make just the movie you want, regardless of how much extra detail you recorded on tape.

This scene plays with modified start and end times.

Here's the current position of the clip.

Drag the slider to advance through the clip quickly, useful for setting marks.

The original clip is not changed, despite edits.

Mark-in time: when the clip starts.

Mark-out time: when the clip stops.

No Fear

Don't worry about experimenting with the trim or split tools. No matter what you do to the clips in your production, the original video you captured and stored on your hard disk (and that appears in the Library list) will never be affected. Only the "copies" of the original that you drag onto the Storyline and use in the video reflect your editing changes.

Imperfect Previews

As you experiment with VideoWave by trimming clips, adding effects, and layering extra audio tracks, you'll discover that the program cannot render all the edits you made to your clips unless you actually produce the movie. If you add an extra audio track, for instance, you won't be able to hear it unless you're in the Audio Studio. To see and hear all your edits, you have to fully render the movie using the **Produce** tool first—as explained in Part 8, "Producing Videotape."

1 Put the Clip in the Viewscreen

To edit a clip, you must first place the scene you want to edit in the Viewscreen. Drag the desired clip from either the Library or the Storyline into the Viewscreen.

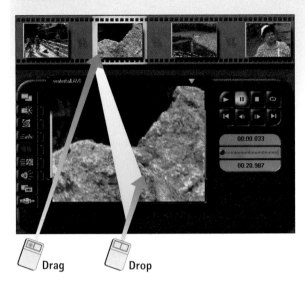

 Drag **Drop**

2 Go to the Cutting Room

Click the **Cutting Room** button. You should see a console of controls appear under the Viewscreen for editing the clip. (If you click this button—or any of the mode selector buttons—by accident, click it again to return to the basic Viewscreen.)

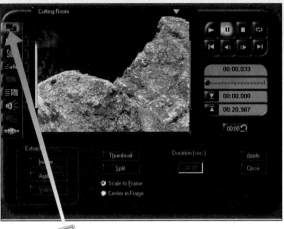

Click

3 Set the Mark-In Point

Use the VCR controls or the brown slider button to set the point where you want the clip to begin. The slider is handy for fine-tuning the exact point at which you want to start. Notice, though, that you can't hear any audio associated with the clip, so you'll have to use visual cues in the clip to know when you're at the right point.

Drag

4 Click the Mark-In Button

After you find the frame at which you want your clip to start, click the **Mark-In** button. This trims video off the front of the clip so that it starts at the point you indicated. Notice that the shortened video clip is also registered in the **Duration** box.

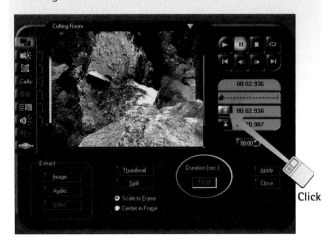

Click

continues

5 Set the Mark-Out Point

Use the VCR buttons or the slider to find the point in the clip at which you want the video to stop playing (the point known as the *mark-out point*).

Drag

6 Click the Mark-Out Button

Click the **Mark-Out** button to lock in this end point for your video. Again, notice that the shortened clip is registered in the **Duration** box.

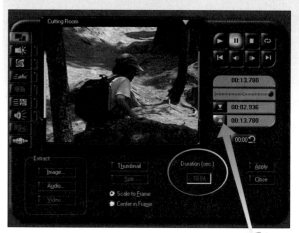

Click

7 Apply the Edit

After marking both the start and end points of your scene, click the **Apply** button. If the clip was already in the Storyline, it is updated with the change. If you dragged the clip to the Viewscreen from the Library, the edited clip is added to the Storyline; the Library clip remains unchanged.

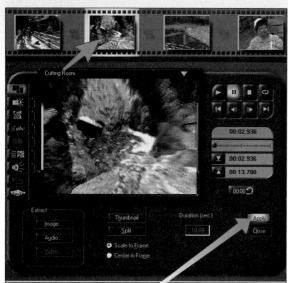

Click

1 Display Clip in the Monitor **P**

Just as you do in VideoWave, you must first add the clip you want to edit to Premiere's **Monitor** window. To do that, double-click a clip in the Timeline.

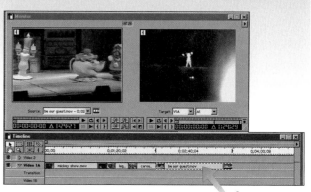

Double-click

2 Set the Mark-In Point P

In the **Source Monitor**, drag the slider around until you reach the frame at which you want the clip to start. Then click the **Mark-In** button to trim the clip to that point.

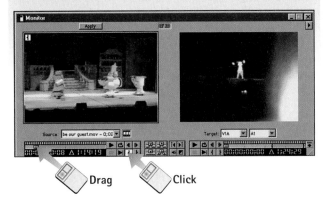

Drag   Click

3 Set the Mark-Out Point P

Now drag the slider to find the point at which you want the clip to stop. Then click the **Mark-Out** button to trim the end of the clip.

Drag   Click

4 Apply the Changes P

Click the **Apply** button at the top of the **Source Monitor**. This causes the changes you made to appear to the clip in the **Timeline**. Remember that the clip in the **Project** window remains unchanged.

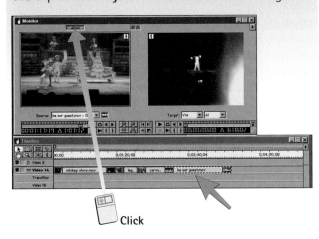

Click

8 Review Your Edits

To view the edited clip, double-click it in either the **Storyline** or the **Timeline** to play the clip. You should see the trimmed version of the original clip.

Double-click

End

How to Split a Clip into Two Scenes

There might be situations in which you want to take a scene you filmed and cut it in half (or into thirds, and so on). By cutting up a scene, you can move different parts of a scene to other places in your movie, or you can perform various tricks or effects on the parts. Splitting a scene is easy and does no permanent damage to the original clip.

Here's the first clip.

Here's the second clip.

The original video is still intact in the Library.

Select where you want to split the clip by dragging the slider.

Click here to split the clip at the selected frame.

Use the Thumbnail Tool

When a clip appears in the Storyline, its first frame is used as a thumbnail to show you the contents of the scene. But if the first frame doesn't really represent most of the action in the clip, you can specify a new thumbnail. Load the clip into the **Cutting Room** and use the slider to display the frame you want to use as a thumbnail. Then click the **Thumbnail** button in the console below the Viewscreen.

1 Go to the Cutting Room

Start by loading your scene (either from the Storyline or the Library) in the Viewscreen and clicking the **Cutting Room** button.

Click

2 Find the Split Point

Drag the slider to find the exact point at which you want to split the scene in two.

Drag the slider to the point you want to split the clip into two scenes.

3 Cut the Scene in Two

Click the **Split** button in the console under the Viewscreen. Note that you can't use the button at the very start or very end of the scene, and there's no need to **Apply** the split—as soon as you click, the two halves appear in the Storyline.

Click

1 Use the Premiere Razor **P**

In Premiere, you can split a scene using the **Razor** tool. Drag the slider until you reach the point in the clip where you want to split it. Then click the **Razor** tool and click the clip to perform the cut. The clip instantly becomes two clips, cut at the point you clicked.

Click

End

How to Add a Transition Between Scenes

Your scenes don't always have to cut suddenly from one to the next. Instead, you can use a variety of *transition effects* to smoothly go from one scene to another over a short period of time. Transitions such as fades and dissolves are very common techniques in the professional world of video production, and you have the same tools at your disposal on the PC.

Here's the old video moving offscreen.

Some effects may look jaggy if they are played too slowly.

Here's the new video coming onscreen.

Library of transition effects.

Transition duration.

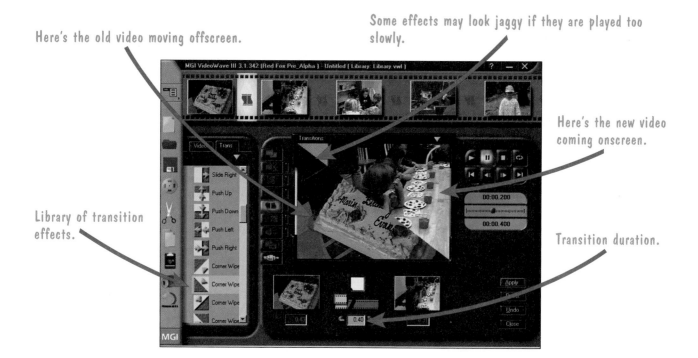

Don't Overuse Them

If you're new to video production, you might feel like a kid in a candy store. All those transitions! Boxes, triangles, circles, barn doors.... The list seems endless. But like someone who sees all the fonts in a page layout program for the first time, you're likely to overdo it and create a video that looks like a kindergartner's art project. Stick to just a few transitions and don't use them between every single scene; plain cuts are okay too.

Borrowing from the Video

When you add a transition effect to segue between two clips, remember that the clips themselves are playing at the same time as the transition. In other words, a movie composed of two one-minute clips is still two minutes long, even with a four-second transition. The transition plays during—and partially obscures—the end of the first clip and the start of the second. Keep that in mind when you preview your film.

1 Go to Transitions

To add a transition in VideoWave, you must enter the Transitions mode. Double-click the **transition placeholder** between two scenes in the Storyline. You should see the Viewscreen change to the Transitions mode.

Double-click

2 Select a Transition

The Library should now display all the transition effects available to you. Double-click a transition (or drag it to the transition box below the Viewscreen). Click the VCR **Play** button to preview the effect. If you're happy with the result, click the **Apply** button to keep the transition in the video. You can later edit the transition (as explained in the next task).

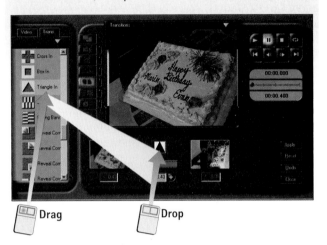

Drag   Drop

1 Alternate Tracks **P**

Premiere uses a very different way of working with transitions. The two clips must be in alternating video tracks in the Timeline, such as **Video 1A** and **Video 1B**. Drag a clip from the **Project** window to the **Video 1A** track, and then drag a second clip to **Video 1B**. Drag the second clip to the right so that it starts just a few seconds before the first clip ends.

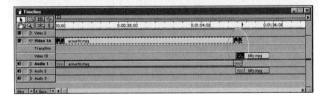

2 Add the Transition **P**

Drag a transition effect from the **Transitions** window and drop it on the **Transition** track in the Timeline. The transition will automatically "snap" to the start of the second clip and the end of the first clip. To preview the effect you just added, drag the work bar so that it is over the transition and then choose **Project, Preview** from the menu.

Drop   Drag

End

How to Modify Transition Settings

The default settings for video transitions are generally quite good, but they might not be exactly what you're looking for. Thankfully, most video editors—including VideoWave and Premiere—offer ways to edit the basic transitions so that you can apply exactly the effect you need for your scenes.

Here's the new video in the transition effect.

Here's the old video going out of view.

Slide the film strip icon to change the transition duration.

Type the duration of the transition in seconds.

The duration of the second scene.

The duration of the first scene.

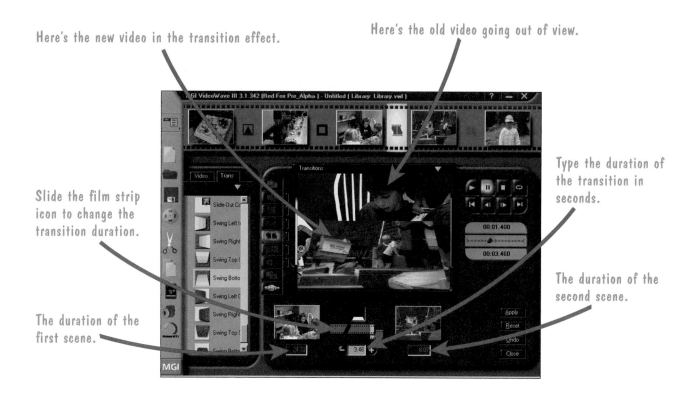

Keep Them Brief

In VideoWave, the only control you have over transitions is their duration. And some videos I've seen capitalize on that, dramatically changing the duration of the transition from one that's so fast you didn't know it happened to one that's several agonizing seconds in length. The reality is that transitions look best when they're rather short, usually just a few seconds or less.

You have to try them out for yourself and decide what looks good. Remember, though, that if your transition is too slow, you'll be able to clearly see lots of jagged edges in your video that give away the fact that it was done on a desktop computer and not in a professional broadcasting studio.

1 Display the Transition

In VideoWave, the only transition option you can change is the duration of the transition. To do that, start by going to Transitions mode—double-click a transition between two scenes in the Storyline.

Double-click

2 Modify the Duration

You can change the duration of the transition by dragging the film strip icons to the left or right, by clicking the plus and minus buttons, or by typing a duration directly into the box. Of course, you cannot specify a transition duration that's longer than the shortest clip.

Drag

3 Preview the Effect

You can get a sense of what the transition will look like by using the VCR controls. Unfortunately, this preview of the transition happens more slowly than it will when it plays back in the final production.

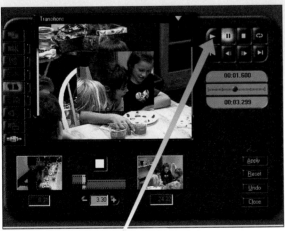

Click

1 Tweak the Settings **P**

In Premiere, many transitions have supplemental controls that change the look of the effect. The most common is the **Border** control. Change the transition options by double-clicking its bar in the Timeline. The **Settings** dialog box opens. If you choose a transition such as the **Band Slide**, you'll see a **Border** slider, which adds a line around the transition effect. Make your changes and click **OK** to apply them to the video.

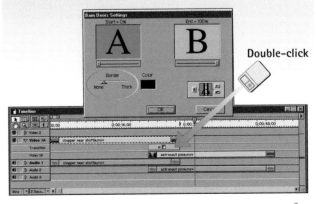

Double-click

End

How to Create a Color Panel

Color panels are plain, single-color backgrounds you can use to start and end your video, display titles against, and do other special effects. VideoWave makes it easy to create such panels for your videos.

Color panels can be added anywhere in the video.

You can add titles to color panels.

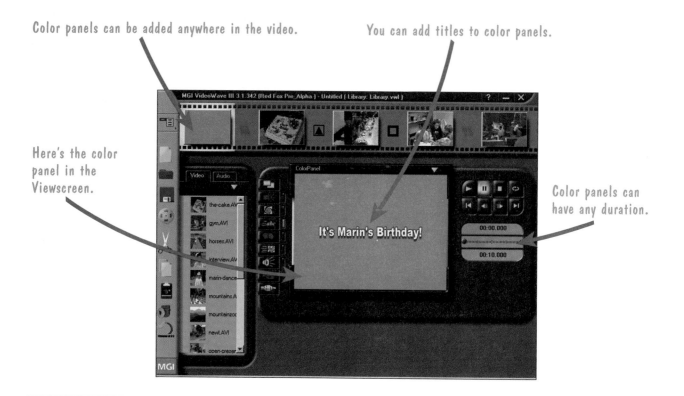

Here's the color panel in the Viewscreen.

Color panels can have any duration.

Make a Color Panel in Premiere

It's easy to make a color panel in Premiere as well. To do that, choose **Project, Create, Color Matte** from the menu. Then choose the color you want and click **OK**. The color panel—or *matte*, in Premiere parlance—appears in the **Project** window. It has a preset duration of one second, but you can drag its duration to any length you desire after it's in the Timeline.

1 Select a Blank Panel

The first step to creating a color panel is to click a blank panel in the Storyline, such as the one at the very end of the video. This panel becomes the color panel, although you can later move it anywhere in the production.

Click

2 Go to the Cutting Room

Click the **Cutting Room** button to get access to editing tools. Although the Viewscreen remains black, be confident that you are working with the panel you selected in the Storyline.

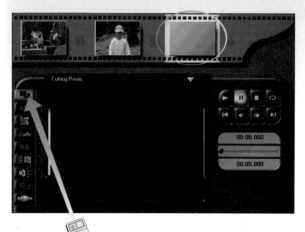

Click

3 Set the Properties

Set the duration of the color panel by typing the time in seconds or by clicking the plus and minus buttons. To choose a color for the panel, click the **Color** button and choose from the millions of shades available. When you have picked the color, click **OK**.

4 Save the Panel

If you want to add the color panel to the Library (so that you can use it again without re-creating it), click the **Image** button in the **Extract** region of the screen. Then click the **Apply** button to add the color panel to the Storyline.

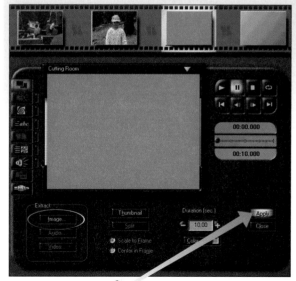

Click

End

How to Superimpose Video

Superimposed video is cool. If not overdone, it's a great way to combine two video clips into one for an MTV-style effect. In VideoWave, not only is it easy to superimpose video, but the program gives you a fair degree of control over the final look of your scene.

Two clips superimposed.

These controls determine when the **Start, Hold,** and **Finish** settings occur to the video.

The video's size, position, and transparency can change through the scene. Use the **Start, Hold,** and **Finish** settings to modify these options.

Video Animator mode.

Use the Image Blend option.

These are the settings for the Foreground video.

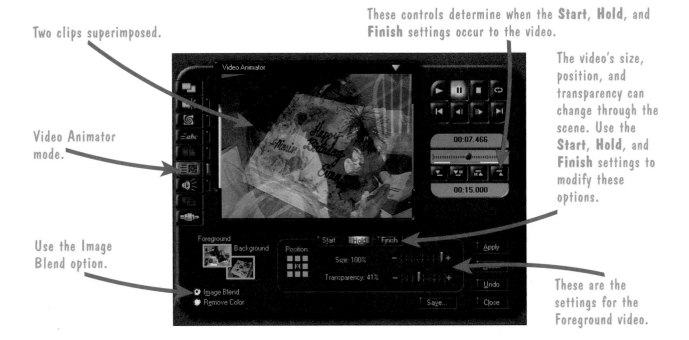

Superimpose Tips

When you superimpose video, it's a good idea to look for clips that complement each other. If both have a lot of action taking place, they can interfere with each other. You might consider muting the color in one clip and perhaps even slowing it down with techniques discussed later in this part of the book. Also, remember that you don't have to superimpose two video clips; you can always lay video over a still image, as I do in this task.

Superimposing in Premiere

You can superimpose video in Premiere as well. To do that, just follow the steps in Task 15, "How to Create Special Effects with a Blue Screen." However, when you open the **Transparency Settings** dialog box, choose **Screen** instead of **Chroma** for your **Key Type.** That's all there is to it!

1 Put the Clip in the Viewscreen

To superimpose two video clips, start by adding the first image—the background image—to the Viewscreen. Drag it there from either the Library or the Storyline.

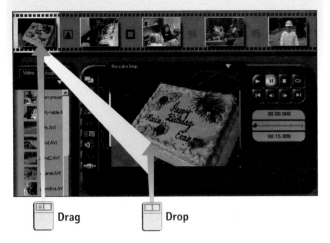

Drag   Drop

2 Size Them Up

In most cases, you'll want both clips to be the same length. To do that, start by checking the length of the background clip. Make a note of its duration.

Clip duration.

3 Trim the Foreground

Drag the foreground clip into the Viewscreen and click the **Cutting Room** button. If you're happy with the length of the two clips, go straight to Step 5. If not, trim the foreground clip (see Task 5, "How to Trim the Length of a Clip") so that it is the same length as the background clip you just measured. Click **Apply** to save your changes to the Storyline.

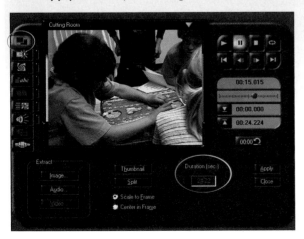

4 Copy to the Library

Although the edited foreground clip is now stored in the Storyline, it doesn't do us a lot of good there. Drag the clip to the Library to store a copy of it there. (You'll have to name the file before it will be copied.)

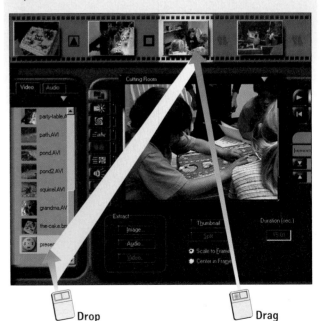

Drop   Drag

continues

5 Load the Background Clip

Now go back to the beginning—load the background clip into the Viewscreen. With all that trimming nonsense out of the way, we're finally ready to superimpose.

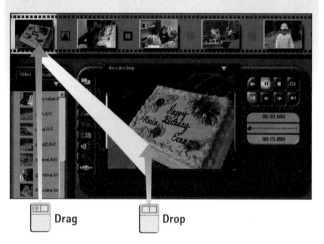

 Drag Drop

6 Go to the Video Animator

Click the **Video Animator** button. In the console area, notice that the loaded clip automatically appears in the **Background** layer.

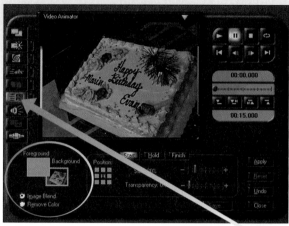

 Click

7 Add the Foreground

Drag the clip you edited for use as the foreground clip from the Library (where you stored it in Step 4) into the Viewscreen. You should see it appear in the **Foreground** layer.

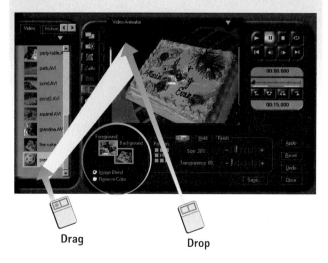

Drag

Drop

8 Select Image Blend

You can do two kinds of video animations: **Image Blend** and **Remove Color**. The **Image Blend** option enables you to mix two layers of video; the **Remove Color** option plays a second video layer on top of any solid color (it is, in effect, a blue screen effect). In this example, make sure that the **Image Blend** option is selected.

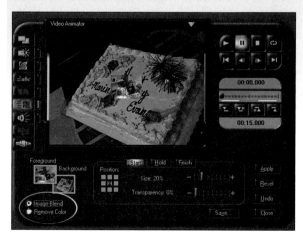

9 Adjust Motion and Transparency

You can make the foreground clip enter the screen from any direction or already be in the middle of the frame at the **Start** of the scene. You can also set the transparency and size of the foreground clip relative to the background clip. Use the **Start**, **Hold**, and **Finish** buttons to change the motion, size, and transparency of the foreground image for the start, middle, and end of the scene. Alternatively, you can use the presets in the Library's **Motion** tab to specify a prebuilt motion for the clip.

10 Edit the Timing

The timing controls under the VCR buttons enable you to specify when the **Start**, **Hold**, and **Finish** effects take place. If you want the entire scene to use the **Hold** position settings, for instance, drag the slider to the extreme left of the clip and click the **Set Beginning of Effect Hold** button. Then drag the slider to the end of the clip and click the corresponding **Set End of Effect Hold** button.

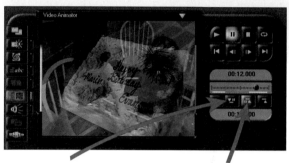

Set Beginning of Effect Hold.   Set End of Effect Hold.

11 Preview Your Scene

At any point, you can get a feel for the effect you've created by playing with the VCR controls and the slider. Move the slider back and forth to see the way the video animation will look.

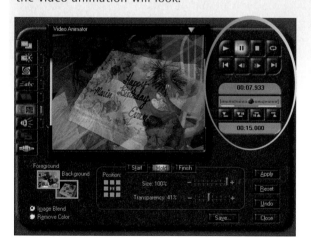

12 Save Your Changes

When you have set up the scene just the way you want it, click the **Apply** button. Your changes will be saved to the Storyline.

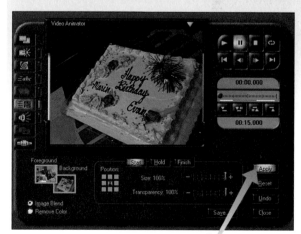

Click

End

How to Add a Video Watermark

Now that you know how to superimpose video clips, let's do something useful. If you watch much television, you've no doubt seen *watermarks* (sometimes called *bugs*). Watermarks are semitransparent graphics that let you know what channel you're watching or who is speaking. You can add your own watermarks to your video productions and look like a real pro.

Save the watermark as a BMP file in any graphics program.

Choose a background color for your watermark that's distinct from the rest of the scene.

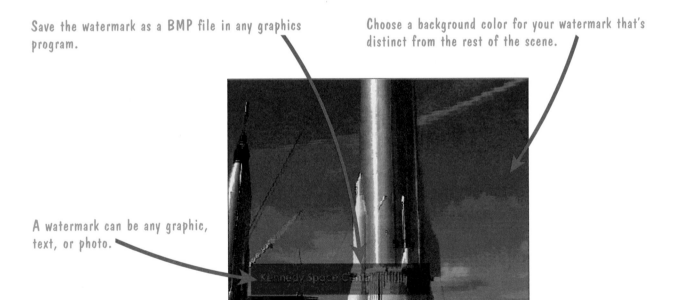

A watermark can be any graphic, text, or photo.

Kennedy Space Center

Watch Your Colors

Watermarks are a cool effect, but they can be tricky. In VideoWave, you have to remove the color from the graphic you're using as a watermark so that your clip shows through. You have to be sure to use a color for your watermark that is distinct from the colors used in the video. When you use the **Tolerance** slider, be sure that you don't overdo it, or you might remove parts of the graphic or video that you want to keep in the finished production.

1 Create the Watermark

You must first create an image in a graphics program such as Photoshop or Paint Shop Pro. Make the image 720×480 pixels in size, a solid color, with some kind of graphic or text in one corner so that it looks like you're making a watermark for CNN. Save it as a **BMP** (Windows bitmap) file.

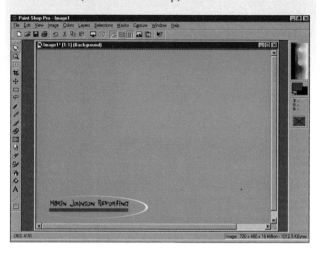

2 Load the Watermark

Click the Library's list menu arrowhead and choose **Add Files**. Find the watermark graphic you created in Step 1 and add it to the Library.

Click

3 Load the Scene

Drag the scene you want to watermark to the Viewscreen from either the Storyline or the Library and then click the **Video Animator** button.

Click

4 Load the Foreground Image

Drag the watermark graphic from the Library into the **Video Animator** screen, where it will become the **Foreground** layer. Also, you probably want to change the watermark's size to 100%.

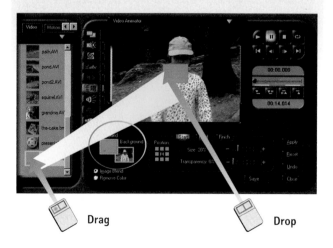

Drag

Drop

continues

5 Remove Color from Graphic

For the watermark to work, you have to "remove" the solid color of the graphic so that the video in the **Background** layer shows through, leaving only the special graphic or text you added. Click the **Remove Color** option.

6 Display the Color Dialog Box

Now that the Video Animator is set to remove color, you have to tell it which color to remove. Start by clicking the **Color** button in the console at the bottom of the screen. The **Color Dialog** box opens.

7 Pick a Color

Click the **Pick a Color** button; the pointer turns into an eyedropper. Move the eyedropper over the graphic in the Viewscreen and click anywhere in the solid region of the graphic to select the color you want to remove from the graphic. Click **OK** to accept the selection.

Click

8 Set the Tolerance

Drag the **Tolerance** slider to the right. You should only have to move it one increment—about 5%—to see the solid color disappear and reveal the video underneath. The graphic bug is all you should now see of the **Foreground** layer. Click **Apply** to save these changes to your video.

Drag

1 Create the Watermark P

If you're watermarking in Premiere, you start the same way you did in VideoWave: Create the graphic in a program such as Photoshop or Paint Shop Pro. Be sure to make the graphic's basic color solid white, however, not some arbitrary color.

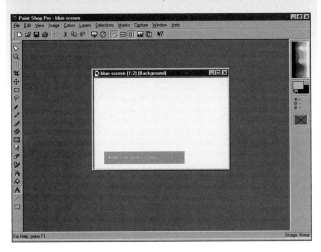

2 Add a New Video Track P

For the watermark to work in Premiere, the Timeline must have a track called **Video 3**. If that track doesn't already exist in the Timeline, click the Timeline list menu arrow and choose **Track Options** to open the **Track Options** dialog box. Click **Add**. In the **Add Tracks** dialog box, make sure that you're adding **1** track and then click **OK** twice to close both dialog boxes.

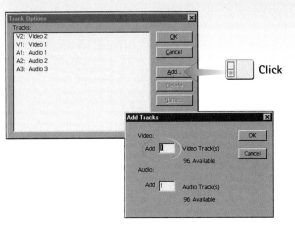

Click

3 Populate the Timeline P

From the **Project** window, drag the video clip to the **Video 2** track and the watermark graphic to the **Video 3** track in the Timeline.

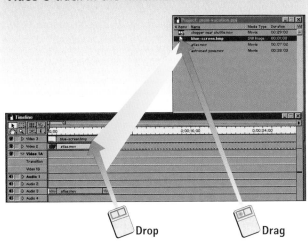

Drop

Drag

4 Use the Track Matte P

Right-click the **Video 2** clip and choose **Video, Transparency** to open the **Transparency Settings** dialog box. From the **Key Type** drop-down list, choose **Track Matte**. The graphic bug should appear on the video.

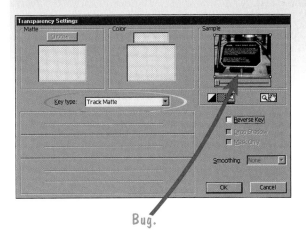

Bug.

End

How to Use Special Effects Filters

Special effects can enhance your movie by distorting video scenes in ways that the viewer won't expect. There are all kinds of filters available, such as swirls, ripples, mosaics, and snow. Using filters, you can make your video look like it's part of a dream sequence, pulled from an old-time TV broadcast, or any of dozens of other effects. It pays to experiment because the possibilities are extensive. Special effects is one area in which Premiere has a leg up on VideoWave—Premiere has more effects, and thanks to an "open architecture," you can buy additional effects as well. Premiere is also more powerful than VideoWave because you can add many layers of video to your movie and perform special effects on each layer. VideoWave restricts you to one layer of effects.

Here's the original video.

Here's the same video with a special "embossed" effect.

Customize Your Effects

By using VideoWave's **Effect Level** slider with the **Start**, **Hold**, and **Finish** buttons, you can create unique effects for your videos. Instead of creating a favorite effect from scratch every time, however, you can click the **Save** button in the **Special Effects** console to store customized effects in the **Custom** tab of the Library.

1   Open the Special Effects

Drag the clip you want to embellish from the Storyline or the Library into the Viewscreen and click the **Special Effects** button. The Special Effects console appears under the Viewscreen and the **Effects** tab pops up in the Library.

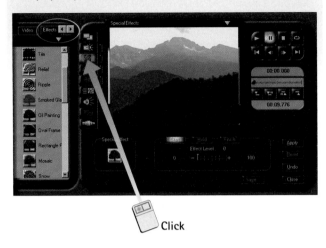

Click

2   Drag an Effect

Find an effect in the Library you want to apply to your video and drag it to the Viewscreen. Experiment with the **Effect Level** slider to vary the intensity of the selected effect.

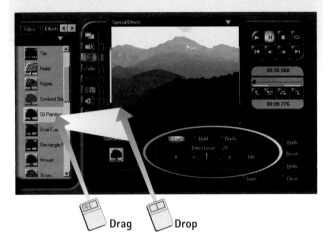

Drag   Drop

3   Set Start, Hold, and Finish

The effect can change intensity at the start, middle, and end of the scene. Click the **Start** button and set the **Effect Level**; repeat for the **Hold** and **Finish** options. When you're done, click the **Apply** button to save the scene to the Storyline.

1   Stack Effects   P

VideoWave doesn't let you apply more than one special effect to a specific clip. If you want, for instance, to render a clip in digital snow and add a wave effect at the same time, you need Premiere. Right-click a clip in the Timeline and choose **Filters** from the shortcut menu. You can add as many filters as you like to the clip—although the processing time becomes enormous if you work with too many effects at once.

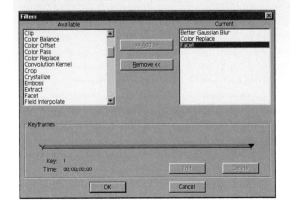

End

How to Color Correct a Scene

In addition to special effects that change your video in very obvious ways, you can use VideoWave's **Darkroom** mode to tweak the color balance. You can be subtle—to adjust for too much red in your video,

for instance—or you can go over the top and burn in a unique color effect (such as the way in which most of the movie *The Matrix* was a lifeless blue).

This Storyline clip is modified; it is not the same as the original file in the Library.

Color changes can be subtle or dramatic.

Darkroom mode.

Drag the preset color filters to the scene.

Customize the color balance of the image here.

Change the brightness and contract of the image here.

Change the saturation of the colors here.

Color Correction in Premiere

If you're using Premiere, the color correction options are found in the same place as the special effects: in the **Filters** dialog box. (Right-click the clip in the Timeline and select **Filters** from the shortcut menu.) In fact, color correction *is* a filter. Because Premiere puts

all these controls in the same place, it's just a matter of adding the color filters you want (such as **Color Balance**, **Color Replace**, or **Black and White**) to the clip and tweaking their settings. There are dozens of color filters in Premiere; see the *Premiere User Guide* for details.

1 Go to the Darkroom

Drag the clip you want to color correct into the Viewscreen and click the **Darkroom** button. A wide variety of color controls and presets appears on the **Filter** tab in the Library.

Click

2 Drag an Effect

You can tweak the color of the clip manually or automatically. If you see a preset that corresponds roughly to the effect you want, drag it from the **Filter** tab of the Library to the Viewscreen. If the color effect is not exactly what you want, you can continue editing the effect in the next step.

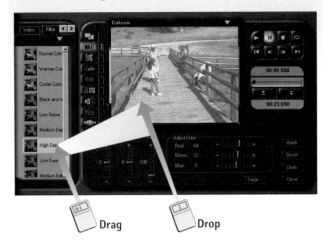

Drag   Drop

3 Fine-Tune the Colors

The **Darkroom** gives you a wide variety of controls for editing color balance. If you want to manually adjust the color levels in the scene, use the **Red**, **Green**, and **Blue** sliders in the **Adjust Color** area. A rule of thumb for increasing the level of one color is to reduce the level of the other two sliders by half as much at the same time.

4 Tweak Color Settings

You can modify the brightness and contrast of the image. In general, you will get the best results by changing both the **Brightness** and **Contrast** controls at the same time because they have an interrelated effect in the picture. The **Color** slider is actually the color saturation—you can enhance colors or bleach them out of the picture using this slider.

End

How to Create Slow-Motion Video

What's more emotional than watching a sports play-back in slow motion? Or the explosive payoff at the end of an action flick in slo-mo? Slow motion is a powerful tool for drawing attention to a key scene.

In this task, you learn how to apply this effect to your own video production by using Premiere; VideoWave does not have a slow-motion option.

The effect of slow motion is easily achieved with Premiere.

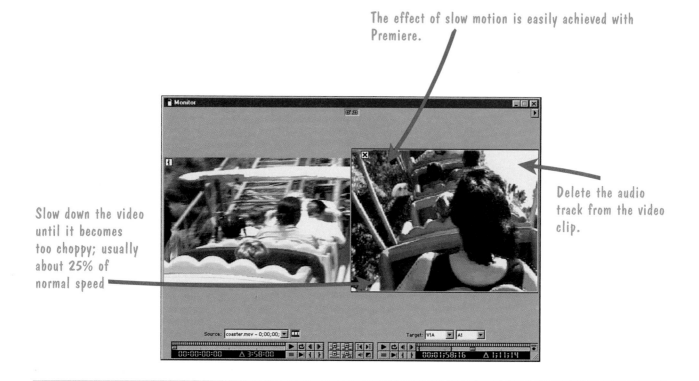

Slow down the video until it becomes too choppy; usually about 25% of normal speed

Delete the audio track from the video clip.

Clever Video Tricks with Premiere

If you want to get fancy with video effects, you're probably ready to make the move from VideoWave to Premiere. Premiere has many more effects than VideoWave does, and they are especially useful if you're trying to be artistic with your video project. For example, one of the Premiere filters enables you to play a video clip (and its sound file) backwards, something that's impossible to do in VideoWave.

1 Fast Shutter Speed **P**

It helps to plan ahead for a slow-motion shot by filming the scene with the fastest shutter speed available on your camcorder—try a setting of 1/500 second. That will give you the best source material.

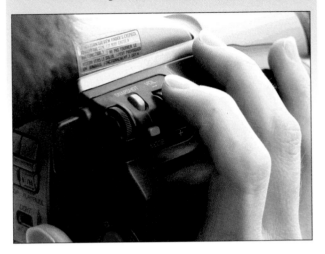

2 Add Clip to Timeline **P**

Drag the clip you want to produce in slow motion from the **Project** window to the Timeline.

3 Set the Playback Speed **P**

Right-click the clip in the Timeline and choose **Speed** from the shortcut menu. In the **Clip Speed** dialog box, set the **New Rate** to a low value such as **25%** or **30%** and click **OK**. Preview the video; if it's too choppy, increase the **New Rate** value using the trial-and-error approach.

Click

4 Delete the Audio **P**

Most of the time, you won't want the audio to play back in slow motion. Click the **Audio** track in the Timeline and press the **Delete** key.

End

How to Create Special Effects with a Blue Screen

In Part 2 of this book, "Working with Your Camcorder," we talked about how to film video with a blue screen background so that you could later overlay a second video source. Now it's time to load that video into your editor and actually replace the blue screen with a second video layer. It's easy to do, and the results can be impressive.

A zoom in on the blue screen can make a clever transition to the next scene.

Here's the background video containing the blue screen.

Here, the edge of blue screen is visible; you can adjust the tolerance levels to eliminate it.

The blue screen does not have to be blue.

The actor is holding a blue screen.

This is the superimposed video on the blue screen.

Watch Your Colors

A blue screen doesn't really have to be blue, as we discussed in Part 2 of the book. In fact, using **chroma key** color removal, you can use a backdrop of any color. Make sure that it's a color unique to the rest of the video background, though, or you might accidentally paint video over parts of the scene where you don't want video—such as the actor's face.

1 Display the Overlay Video

Find the video that you want to show through the blue screen and add it to the Viewscreen. If you were blue-screening the starfield on a Star Trek bridge, for instance, this would be the star pattern or a Klingon warship.

2 Go to the Video Animator

Click the **Video Animator** button to begin editing the video layers. Notice that the video you have loaded is automatically assigned to the **Background** layer in the console.

Click

3 Add the Blue Screen Clip

Now drag the clip that actually contains the blue screen into the **Video Animator** screen. This video clip becomes the **Foreground** layer in the console. You should see that the clip doesn't actually fill the screen; that's because the size of the clip defaults to **20%** in the **Start** and **Finish** steps of the scene. Drag the **Size** slider all the way to **100%** and then click the **Finish** button and drag the **Size** slider to **100%** again. Click the **Start** button so that you're working at the beginning of the clip again.

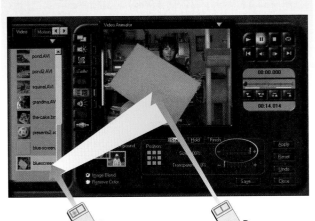

Drag

Drop

4 Switch to Remove Color Mode

By default, the VideoWave Video Animator is set to **Image Blend** mode. Click the **Remove Color** option to enable the chroma key effect that we need for this shot.

Click

continues

How to Create Special Effects with a Blue Screen   97

5 Pick the Blue Screen Color

Now we need to remove the blue screen from the scene so that we can see through to the other video layer. Click the **Color** button and then click the **Pick a Color** button. Click anywhere in the blue screen to select the color you're removing and then click **OK**.

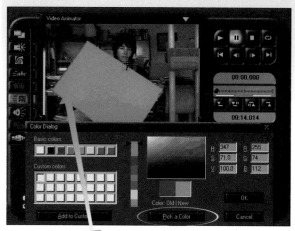

Click

6 Increase the Tolerance

Drag the **Tolerance** slider to the right until the blue screen disappears and is replaced by the **Background** layer video (the overlay video), but stop dragging the slider before the overlay video spills into the rest of the scene.

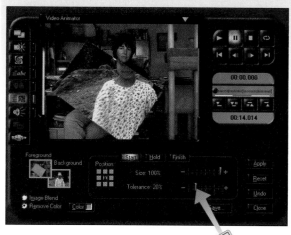

Drag

7 Apply Your Changes

To finish the blue screen effect, click the **Apply** button. The scene is updated in the Storyline.

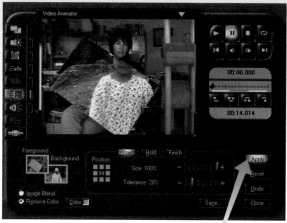

Click

1 Add the Overlay P

The process of creating a blue screen overlay in Premiere is a little different. Start by dragging the overlay video—the clip that you want to appear in the blue screen—from the **Project** window to the **Video 1A** track in the Timeline.

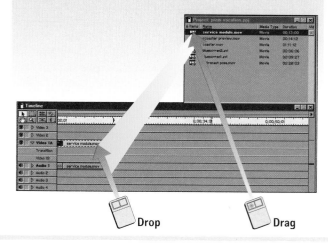

Drop   Drag

2 Add the Blue Screen **P**

Drag the background video clip (the clip that contains the blue screen) from the **Project** window to the **Video 2** track in the Timeline.

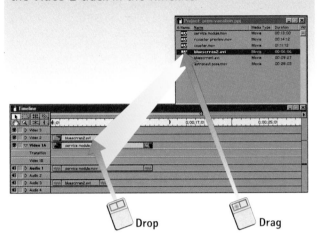

Drop

Drag

3 Open the Transparency Box **P**

Right-click the blue screen clip in the **Video 2** track and choose **Video, Transparency**. The **Transparency Settings** dialog box opens.

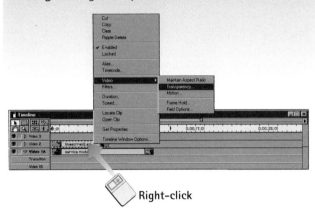

Right-click

4 Switch to Chroma Key **P**

From the **Key type** drop-down list, choose **Chroma**. Then click the blue screen in the **Color** pane to select the color you are going to replace with the overlay video.

Click

5 Increase the Similarity **P**

The **Similarity** slider in Premiere is equivalent to the **Tolerance** slider in VideoWave. Drag the **Similarity** slider to the right until the blue screen in the **Sample** pane is filled with the overlay video, but stop before that video spills into the rest of the background scene. Click the **OK** button when you're done.

Drag

End

How to Preview Your Movie on the Computer

Now that you know the basics for editing a movie, you can actually put together a simple film. We haven't discussed titling or audio tricks yet (you'll learn about those aspects of video editing in later parts in the book), but you might be ready to combine some clips and see what they look like. You don't even have to dump the scenes to tape to see them play; in this task, you'll learn how to preview your movie on the computer screen.

Shift-select the panels you want to preview.

Use the VCR controls to play the preview.

The preview appears in the Viewscreen.

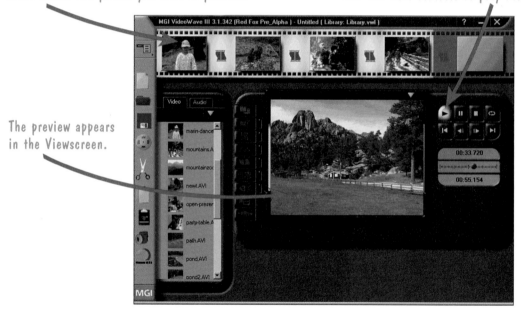

Save Early, Save Often

You should save your work often—and especially before previewing your movie. Although you shouldn't necessarily expect your PC to crash, an editing program such as VideoWave or Premiere can really tax your computer. Generating a preview file could cause your computer to experience a software error—which would be bad if you haven't saved any of your work.

1 Shift-Select

To preview your VideoWave production on the PC, start by clicking the first panel in the Storyline that you want to see. Then, holding down the **Shift** key on the keyboard, click the final panel you want to include in the preview. All the intermediate panels should be highlighted.

Click   **⬆Shift**   Click

2 Play the Movie

Right-click the selected panels and choose **Preview** from the shortcut menu. The preview might drop some frames—especially if you are using transitions or filters—but they'll all play properly later, when you record the movie to tape. Alternatively, use the VCR controls to play the video.

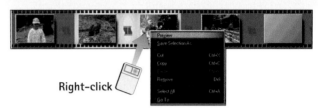

Right-click

1 Select a Region [P]

In Premiere, the **work area bar** is located at the top of the Timeline. Drag the bar to the left or right until it encompasses all the video you want to watch.

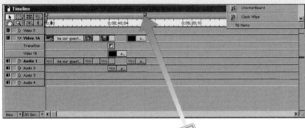

 Drag

2 Preview the Movie [P]

Choose **Project, Preview** from the menu bar. If you haven't yet saved this project, Premiere prompts you to do that. Then Premiere writes the movie to your hard drive and plays it. It can take several minutes or even several hours to generate the preview, so be patient.

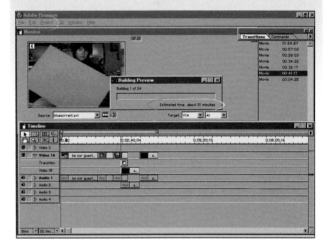

End

Task

5

Working with Titles

*N*o video is complete without some *titles*—text that can leap or fade or dance or spin its way onto the screen to identify your movie or specific scenes. Titles help your viewer immediately understand the context of your movie, and they add a professional touch to your production as well.

Actually, don't think that the only text in your video must be a traditional title scene at the beginning of the film; you can also create captions, credits, and even subtitles! Most people save the credit roll for the end of the movie. *Credits* can mention who filmed, produced, and otherwise slaved over your film. Credits also identify who appeared in the film and what music you used. Just watch a Hollywood movie all the way to the end for some ideas about who to include in your credits. Captions and subtitles are also handy text tools to use in your production. *Captions* can label a scene or identify a location or person onscreen. *Subtitles*, of course, translate foreign-language dialog or transcribe hard-to-understand speech.

Video editors such as VideoWave and Premiere enable you to use text as a different kind of special effect, complete with colors, transparency, and motion. In this part of the book, I show you how to master text and title tools in both of these programs. ●

How to Add Titles to a Video

The most basic text effect you can add to a video is the traditional title shot. Titles can cut on and off the screen; you can also use an animation technique to make the title appear and disappear. In this task, we'll start simple and just get the titles into your video.

Title.

Titles are usually a contrasting color.

Make titles large, don't use thin fonts.

Titles can appear on video, still images, or color panels.

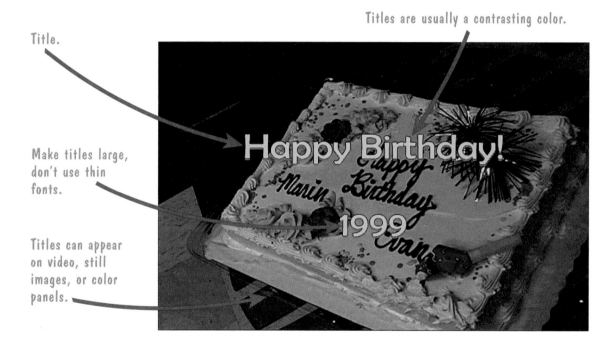

A Tale of Two Titles

As you might expect, Premiere enables you to make significantly more sophisticated titles than VideoWave—but at a cost. It takes more effort and expertise to make your video in Premiere. On the bright side, 90% of all the titling effects you can do in Premiere are also available in VideoWave, so feel free to stick with the simpler program for most, if not all, your video projects. If you run into a text effect that there's simply no way to do in VideoWave (such as text that flies in four directions at once), remember that you can always turn to Premiere.

1 Display the Video

The title has to be displayed on top of something such as a video clip or a color panel. Choose a background for your title and add it to the Viewscreen. In this example, I selected a video clip of a birthday cake from the list of clips and dragged it to the Viewscreen.

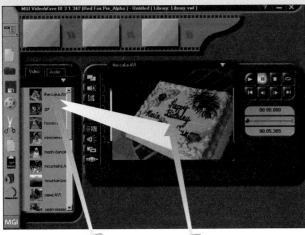

Drag   Drop

2 Open the Text Animator

VideoWave uses a module called the **Text Animator** to add titles to your productions. Click the **Text Animator** button.

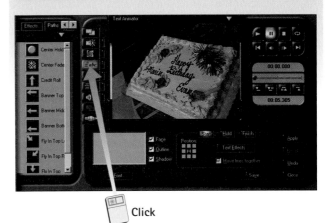

 Click

3 Type the Title

In the text box, type the title you want to give your video. Press the **Enter** key to arrange the title on to multiple lines. Keep in mind that the text box doesn't show the text's true appearance. You have to look on the Viewscreen to see what your finished titles really look like.

4 Apply the Changes

When your title is complete, click the **Apply** button to add the titles to the clip and update the changes to the Storyline.

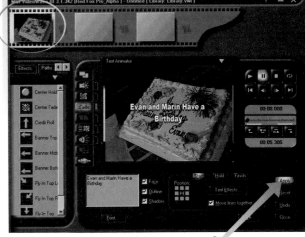

Click

continues

1 Create a Blank Title P

In Premiere, titles are clips that can be displayed on their own or over any other clip. Start by choosing **File, New, Title** from the menu. The title window opens.

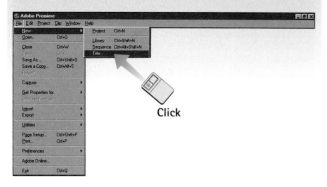

Click

2 Choose a Sample Clip P

It can help if you use some video in the background of the title. The video won't be a part of the title, but it will help you position and format the title. Double-click a clip to add it to the **Source Monitor** window.

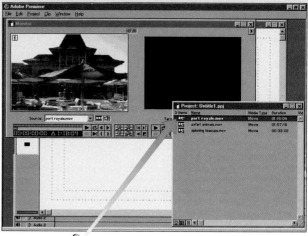

Double-click

3 Choose a Frame P

If you want the first frame of the clip to be your background, drag it from the **Monitor** window to the title window. If not, use the slider to find the frame you want to use and then choose **Clip, Set Marker, 0** from the menu. Then drag the desired clip from the **Monitor** window to the title window. This process can help you see what the titles will look like over the final video, but remember that the video you add here isn't really a part of the title file.

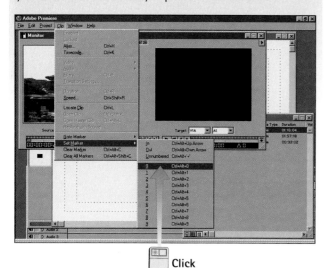

Click

4 Type the Title P

Click the **Text** tool in the title window palette and click in the title window to position the insertion point. Type the text that will be your title. You can modify the look of the titles using options in the **Title** menu, as described in the following task.

5 Save the Title Clip P

Now save the title clip by choosing **File, Save As** from the menu. Give the title clip a name and click **Save**. Note that the default extension for a Premiere title file is **PTL**.

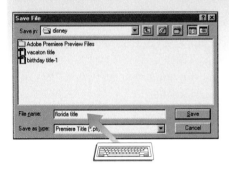

6 Close the Title Window P

Click the close box in the title window's toolbar to get rid of the **Title** window.

Click

7 Load the Title Clip P

Now it's time to add the title to the project. Right-click the **Project** window and choose **Import, File**. The **File Open** dialog box appears; find the title file and click to select it.

Click

8 Add the Title to the Timeline P

Now drag the title file from the **Project** window to the **Timeline**. If you want to continue editing the title, double-click the filename in the **Project** window to reopen the title window.

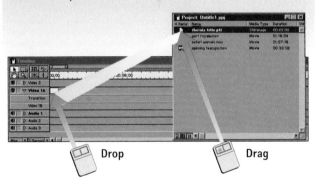

Drop   Drag

End

How to Color and Size Your Titles

In the last task, you learned how to make a very basic title—it appears onscreen in a rather ordinary-looking font and it stays there until the scene is over.

Let's start making our titles a little fancier—the first step is with color and styles. In this task, I'll show you how to change the appearance of your titles in both VideoWave and Premiere.

You can control color, outline, and shadow.

Use title case (capitalize the first letter of each word) when writing titles.

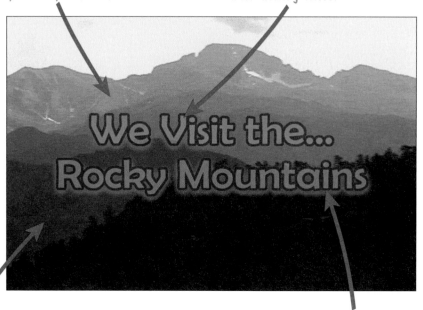

Title backgrounds should usually be visually simple.

Keep the font simple for readability.

Readability Is Paramount

The most important thing about your titles is that the audience should be able to read them. Consider these tips when making titles:

- They should be big. Don't use tiny characters, or people will have to put their noses up to the screen to see them.

- Don't use thin fonts. Thicker is better—thin fonts tend to be hard to read on television screens.

- Use high-contrast colors. Choose your colors based on the video behind the text. The color of the text should stand out for added visibility.

- Leave the titles onscreen longer. Longer than what? Longer than you think they need to be onscreen. Recognize the fact that many people read slower than you do.

1   Open the Text Animator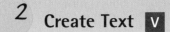

To edit the text characteristics of your title, start by opening the title scene in the **Text Animator**. To do that, drag the title scene video clip to the Viewscreen and click the **Text Animator** button.

Click

2   Create Text

Type the text of your title in the text box.

3   Select a Font

Click the **Font** button under the text box to display the **Font** dialog box. Choose a font, style, and size. Click **OK** to see what the title looks like with this font selection; return to the **Font** dialog box if you want to make any changes. Notice that you can also align the text to the left or right margin or center it in the screen.

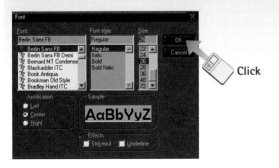

Click

4   Change Text Color

To change the color of the title, click the **Effects** tab in the **Library** and double-click a color style that appeals to you.

Double-click

continues

5 Edit the Text Effect V

To the right of the text box are checkboxes for **Face** (the main, thick part of each character), **Outline** (the line that wraps around each character), and **Shadow** (the backdrop that makes each character stand out from the video). You can turn these elements of the title on or off by clicking the checkboxes.

6 Customize the Text Effect V

If you prefer, you can tweak the text effects by clicking the **Text Effects** button in the **Text Animator** console. The **Text Effects** dialog box enables you to change the color and intensity of the face, outline, and shadow of the text. Note that you can make this effect change over time by setting different values for **Start**, **Hold**, and **Finish** (click each of these buttons, located above the **Text Effects** button, and specify settings). When you're done, click the **Apply** button to save these changes to your video.

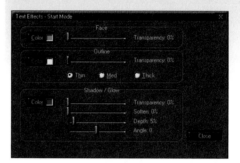

1 Enter Text P

Premiere gives you much more control over the text, but the program is not as convenient to use as VideoWave. Start by entering some title text in the Premiere screen as explained in the last task.

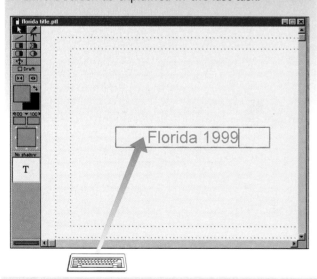

2 Select the Text P

Perhaps the biggest difference between VideoWave and Premiere is that Premiere enables you to change title attributes on a character-by-character basis; with VideoWave, you change all the text at once. Double-click in the text box and then select the text you want to change.

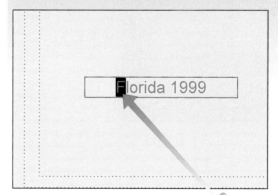

 Double-click

3 Choose a Font [P]

With the appropriate text selected, choose **Title, Font** from the menu. In the **Font** dialog box that opens, select the font, style, and size that you like. Click **OK** to close the dialog box and apply your font choices.

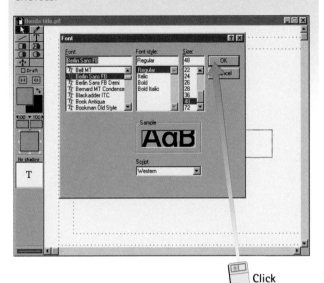

Click

4 Size Quick Pick [P]

You don't have to open the **Font** dialog box to pick a font size; you can also select the text to edit and then choose **Title, Size**, and the desired font size from the menu.

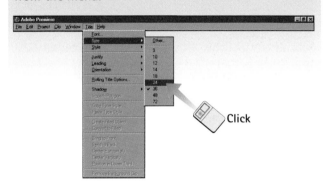

Click

5 Choose a Color [P]

If you want, each character in your title can be a different color. Select the desired text and then click the color box at the left side of the window. A **Color Picker** dialog box appears, from which you can choose a color for the selected text.

6 Choose a Color from a Clip [P]

If you prefer, you can pick a color for the text directly from the sample clip behind the text. To do that, click the **Eyedropper** tool in the palette and then click a spot in the video clip.

Click

End

How to Make Titles Roll

It's almost a cliché, it's so common: Titles tend to move around on the screen. Sometimes they *roll*—go from the top to the bottom of the screen—and sometimes they crawl. But no matter what you want to do to your video text, the technique is easy to accomplish with VideoWave.

Preset paths for your title.

Title is static in **Hold** position here.

Title starts to move to **Finish** position here.

Title enters from lower-right corner.

Control the Flow

Depending on how you use the **Mark-In** and **Mark-Out** points for text animation, you can get radically different effects. Consider some of these tips:

- If you want the text to hover onscreen, set the **Hold Mark-In** and **Hold Mark-Out** points a few seconds apart.

- If you want the titles to roll smoothly without stopping, make the **Hold Mark-In** and **Hold Mark-Out** points identical.

- If you want the titles to speed onto the screen but scroll off slowly, make the **Hold** point closer to the start of the clip. Likewise, put the **Hold** point closer to the end of the clip to make the titles move in slowly but leave quickly.

1 Choose a Preset Path V

The easiest way to make text roll is to use a preset path. Load the scene that you want to appear behind the titles. Click the **Text Animator** button if necessary and then click the **Paths** tab in the **Library**. Double-click the **Credit Roll** option. Click the **Play** button in the VCR controls to preview the effect. If you like it, just click **Apply**.

Double-click

2 Set a Start Position V

If you want to create a custom path (for example, a motion that goes from the bottom-right corner to the top-left corner), use the **Start**, **Hold**, and **Finish** buttons to make these selections. Click **Start** and then click the bottom-right position in the 9-block grid. This setting makes the text start offscreen at the bottom-right corner when the scene begins.

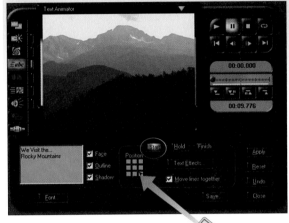

Click

3 Set the Hold Position V

Where do you want the text to be halfway through the scene? In the middle of the screen, in this case. Click the **Hold** button and then click the center position in the grid.

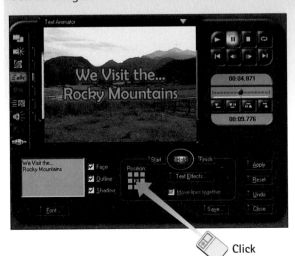

Click

4 Set the Finish V

At the end of the scene, the text should scroll off the top left of the screen. Click the **Finish** button and then click the top-left corner of the **Position** grid.

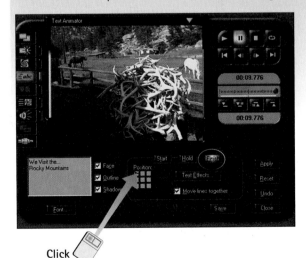

Click

continues

5 Edit the Path Duration V

We've set the motion of the text, but not the timing. Use the **Mark-In** and **Mark-Out** buttons to specify when the three motion phases occur. These buttons appear under the VCR controls and enable you to set when the effect should begin, when the effect should hold in the middle of the scene, and when the effect should end.

6 Apply the Changes V

With the path of the text set, click the **Apply** button. Click the **First Frame** button and then the **Play** button in the VCR controls to see what your rolling title looks like now.

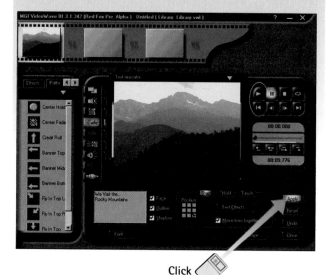

Click

1 Select Rolling Titles P

Premiere doesn't have drag-and-drop preset paths for titles to follow, but it's easy to create moving titles nonetheless. Click the **Rolling Title** tool in the tool palette. This tool enables you to create a text region within which the text rolls.

2 Create a Text Box P

In the title window, click and drag the **Rolling Title** tool to create a region in which the title rolls.

Drag

3 Enter Text P

Click in the text region and type a title. If you want, you can adjust the font size and type from the **Title** menu.

4 Add Dead Space P

Now add hard returns (press **Enter**) before and after the title so that the text scrolls properly. It might take some experimentation to get the number of hard returns right.

Press Enter before and after title.

5 Select a Path P

Right-click the text box and choose **Rolling Text Options** from the shortcut menu. In the dialog box that appears, select **Move Down** as the movement you want the text to take and click **OK**.

Right-click

6 Test Your Title Roll P

Click and drag the slider in the lower-left corner of the title window. Using this slider, you can test the motion of your titles and add more space before or after the text as needed to get the effect you want.

End

How to Make Titles Crawl

In video lingo, a *crawl* is text moving across the screen—from side to side—as opposed to a *roll*—which is text moving from top to bottom. In the last task, you learned how to make titles move, so the crawl is a piece of cake.

Banner paths make text crawl.

This title moves to the left.

Title starts offscreen on right.

This bar indicates that the title will "hold" in the center of the screen for a few seconds.

Don't Always Use CG

Your titles don't have to be character-generated text—that is, done on the PC. You can use props and scenery for more natural-looking or clever titles. Consider filming street signs, for instance, and using them when appropriate for titles. You can even film a traffic sign and digitally alter the text on the sign in a program such as Paint Shop Pro or Photoshop—the resulting graphic can be a great title.

Did you ever see the video for Bob Dylan's classic song, *Subterranean Homesick Blues*? Just holding up a cardboard sign with words on it has its charms.

1 Choose the Path V

With a clip loaded in the **Text Animator**, double-click one of the banner paths from the **Library**. All the banner paths move text across the screen; the speed of the crawl depends on the length of the clip and how much text you need to move.

Double-click

2 Set the Timing V

Use the timing controls under the VCR buttons to modify the flow of the text. By default, banner crawls move smoothly from one side to the other, but you can make them hover in the middle of the screen by using the **Hold Mark-In** and **Hold Mark-Out** buttons. You can also change the text attributes at various locations along the crawl path using the **Start**, **Hold**, and **Finish** buttons and the **Text Effects** button.

1 Create Rolling Text P

Click Premiere's **Rolling Text** tool and drag a horizontal text box on top of the video clip you want to use for the background of your title. Right-click in the text box and choose **Rolling Title Options** from the shortcut menu. In the dialog box that appears, select the **Move Left** or **Move Right** option to direct the motion of the text and click **OK**.

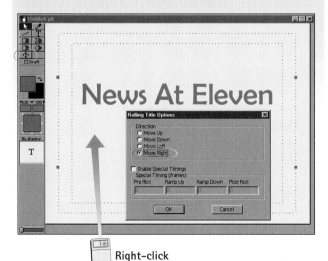

Right-click

2 Massage the White Space P

Type the text for your title and adjust the font, size, and color of the text. Press the **Spacebar** enough times so that you add a screen's worth of space on both sides of the text. Test the crawl using the slider at the bottom of the Title window.

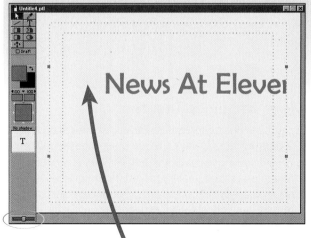

Press **Spacebar** to add spaces before and after the title.

End

How to Make Credits Roll

A credit roll is actually pretty similar to a title roll; both involve text moving across the screen. A credit roll, however, moves a lot more text than does a title roll. Typically, you want to include a credit roll at the end of a movie to give credit where credit is due—to yourself, the people who appear in the film, the music, and so on. Watch the end of a Hollywood movie for a peek at what professional credits look like. This task explains how to create a credit roll for yourself.

This path makes text roll up the screen.

Speed is determined by the length of the clip or color panel.

The spacebar and Enter key are the only tools you can use to format text in a credit roll.

Start and Finish positions are automatically set by double-clicking the path.

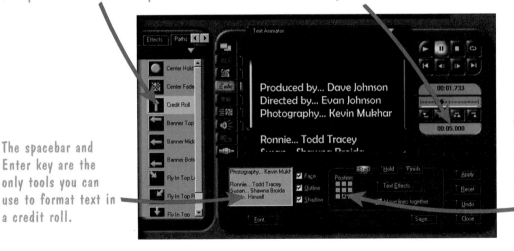

Move the Lines Together

You have probably seen the option in the **Text Animator** console called **Move lines together**. When it's enabled, it keeps all the text moving as a group, regardless of how many separate lines (and hard returns) are in the text. When it's disabled, each line of text moves onscreen independently, one after the other. Although you generally wouldn't want to direct the movements of each line separately in a credit roll, disabling the **Move lines together** option can be effective if you're displaying titles at the beginning of a film—experiment for yourself. Unfortunately, you have no control over how those lines move—it's all preset. To exact precise control over title movement, see the How-To Hints in Task 7, later in this part, which use Premiere to do some fancy titling.

1 Create a Color Panel

Most credit sequences occur on a blank background, typically black. Although you can roll credits over video if you want to, for this example, create a color panel and load it into the Viewscreen: Right-click the last blank clip in the Storyline and select **Create Color Panel**. From the console at the bottom of the screen, pick a color for the panel. Keep in mind that the credits will roll as quickly or as slowly as necessary to display completely within the duration of the color panel, so adjust the **Duration** setting accordingly.

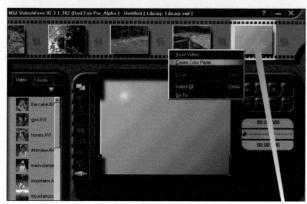

 Right-click

2 Open the Text Animator

Click the **Text Animator** button.

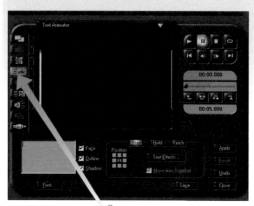

 Click

3 Type the Credits

Type the text for your credits. Most credits are left justified (click the **Font** button and make sure that the **Left** option is selected). Unfortunately, VideoWave doesn't allow you to line up text using tabs, so you might have to be creative to get an effect you like.

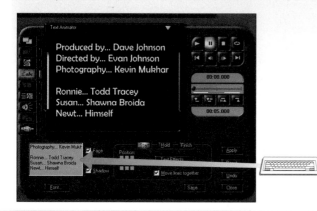

4 Choose the Credit Roll Path

In the **Library**, double-click the **Credit Roll** path. Preview the credits by using the VCR buttons in the Preview Control Panel and click **Apply** when you're done. Remember that you might need to adjust the duration of the color panel based on how quickly you want the credits to roll across the screen.

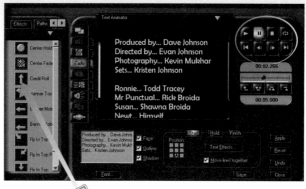

 Double-click

End

How to Add Captions and Subtitles to a Scene

Captions and subtitles are more kinds of titling that you can easily do with your video editor. Both of these text formats are a little different from titles and credits in that they traditionally don't move; they appear in place on the screen, linger for a few moments, and then leave. This task shows how to create captions and subtitles in VideoWave.

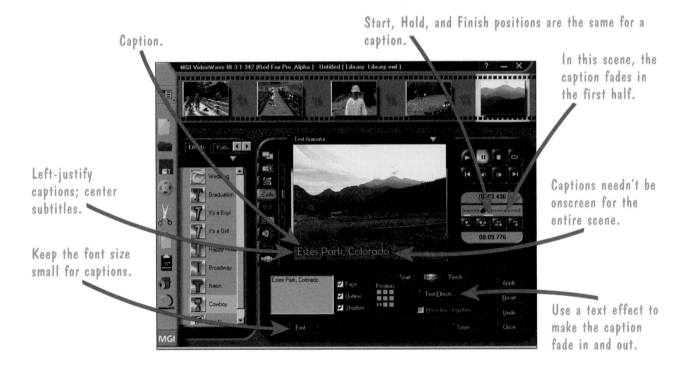

Caption.

Start, Hold, and Finish positions are the same for a caption.

In this scene, the caption fades in the first half.

Left-justify captions; center subtitles.

Captions needn't be onscreen for the entire scene.

Keep the font size small for captions.

Use a text effect to make the caption fade in and out.

Why Use Captions?

Captions can come in handy. Here are a few reasons why you might want to use them:

- Label people who have just entered a scene.
- Describe the location.

- Translate hard-to-understand or foreign speech.
- Explain what is going on in a scene, such as "This is the final race for the Pinewood Derby championship."

1 Load the Scene

Start by dragging the scene to which you want to add captions into the view screen.

2 Go to the Text Animator

Click the **Text Animator** button to switch to the text mode.

Click

3 Add the Caption

In the text box, type the caption or subtitle you plan to use for this clip. What the text looks like is up to you, but I recommend sticking with a simple, easy-to-read font. Avoid special effects—they're distracting in captions. Captions should be functional, not decorative.

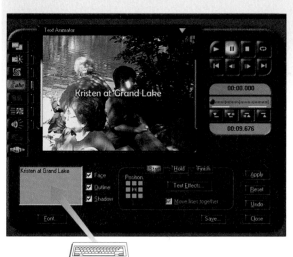

4 Set the Start Position

Most often, you'll find captions in the lower-left corner of the screen. (Subtitles, on the other hand, are usually centered at the bottom of the screen.) Click the **Start** button and click the lower-left box in the **Position** grid to identify this as the location where you want the caption to first appear.

Click

continues

5 Set the Hold Position

Because we don't want the caption to move, click the **Hold** button and click the lower-left box in the **Position** grid to ensure that the title stays in that position through the middle of the video clip. Remember that the length of the Hold portion of the video is determined by the middle two buttons under the VCR controls.

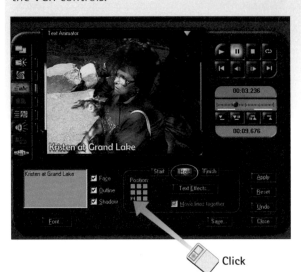

Click

6 Set the Finish Position

Click the **Finish** button and again click the lower-left box in the **Position** grid. Now the caption won't move through the entire course of the scene.

Click

7 Set the Timing

Now you need to decide when the caption appears and leaves the scene. Drag the brown button on the slider on the right side of the screen until you see the frame where you want to start the caption in the view screen. Click the **Hold Mark-In** button. Drag the brown button until you see the frame where you want the text to disappear and click the **Hold Mark-Out** button. The red Hold line shows you how long the caption will remain onscreen.

Drag

8 Start the Fade In

The text of the caption should fade in from the Start mark to the Hold mark. To set VideoWave to do this, click the **Start** button and then click the **Text Effects** button. Drag all three **Transparency** sliders to **100%** and click **Close**. (Text that is 100% transparent at the start of the clip won't be seen; it will fade into sight by the time the clip hits the Hold mark.)

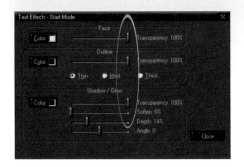

9 Verify the Hold Effect

Click the **Hold** button and click the **Text Effects** button. Make sure that the **Transparency** sliders are set to **0%**, **0%**, and **50%**. Click **Close**. (Text that is 0% transparent is solid; a 50% transparent Shadow/Glow effect highlights the text nicely. The solid text appears onscreen when the clip hits the first Hold mark and remains onscreen for the duration of the Hold.)

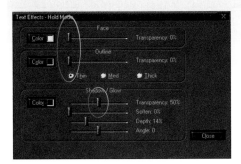

10 Finish the Fade Out

The text should fade out from the end of the Hold to the Finish mark. Click the **Finish** button and then click the **Text Effects** button. Drag all three **Transparency** sliders to **100%**, just as you did for the Start of the clip, and click **Close**.

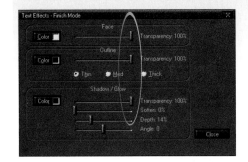

11 Preview the Caption

Use the VCR buttons to preview the effect of the caption. Make sure that the caption appears and disappears when you want it to during the scene.

12 Apply Your Changes

That's it! Click the **Apply** button to update the scene in the Storyline with the caption.

Click

End

How to Move Text in Two Directions at Once

How can you create some really snazzy titles that grab your audience's eyes? How about making text fly into the scene from different directions?

VideoWave isn't really designed to do that, but here's a technique for doing it that's simple but effective.

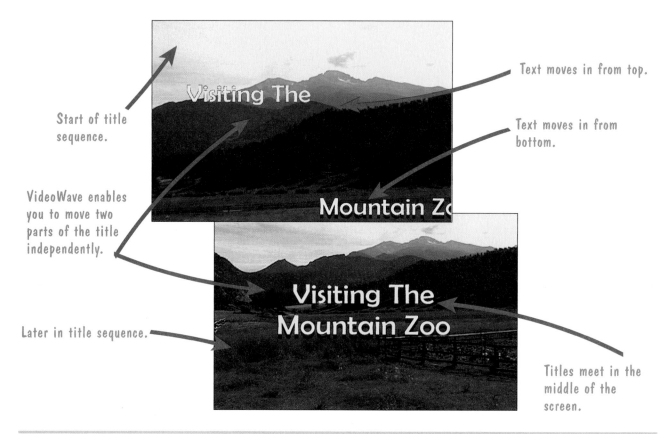

Start of title sequence.

Text moves in from top.

Text moves in from bottom.

VideoWave enables you to move two parts of the title independently.

Later in title sequence.

Visiting The Mountain Zoo

Titles meet in the middle of the screen.

Getting Lots of Text Animation

VideoWave is a powerful program, but it simply can't do some really advanced stuff—such as making four different titles fly into the scene from different directions at once. To do that, you need Premiere. Follow this outline to make four phrases move in from the four edges of the screen and meet near the middle of the screen:

- Set each box to exhibit the movement you want the text in that box to make: up, down, left, or right. Make sure that each box touches the side of the screen from which the text will fly in—that way, the text will appear to enter from offscreen.

- Use the **Enable Special Timings** option in the **Rolling Title Options** dialog box to synchronize the different title movements. By changing the timing value in this dialog box, you change the rate at which the text moves with respect to other text elements on the screen. In other words, text can enter at different speeds.

1 Create a Color Panel

To have two independent titles moving in one scene, you must have two layers: the video and a transparent color panel. Start by creating a color panel; leave it black.

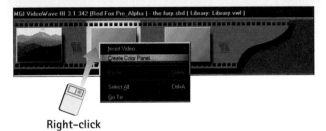

Right-click

2 Set the Duration

The panel must have a duration that's the same as the video clip that plays behind it. If you don't know the duration of the clip, drag it into the Viewscreen and check the duration under the VCR controls. In the **Cutting Room** console, set the duration for the color panel based on the clip.

3 Type the Title

Click the **Text Animator** button. In the text box, type the part of the title that will be displayed and animated in this panel. (In this example, I typed the top line of my two-line title; the second line of the title will be created on the video clip itself.)

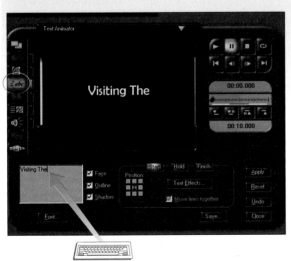

4 Set the Motion

With an eye on what the finished product will look like, use the **Start**, **Hold**, and **Finish** buttons and the **Position** grid to set the motion of the text. You might want one line to roll from the top and stop in the middle, while another line rolls from the bottom and stops in the middle, just under the top word. In a situation like this one, you might have to add a hard return or two above the text that comes up from the bottom so that the two titles don't crowd each other.

continues

5 Apply the Changes

Click the **Apply** button to save this color panel and its text to the Storyline.

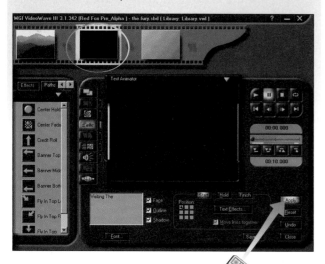

Click

6 Put It in the Library

To use this color panel in the **Video Animator**, the panel must exist in the **Library**. Drag it from the Storyline to the Library (click the **Cutting Room** mode selector button if necessary to see the **Video** tab); when prompted by the **Save As** dialog box, give the color panel and its title a filename.

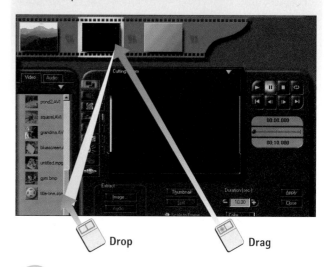

Drop   Drag

7 Open the Video Clip

Drag the video clip on which you want the titles to actually appear from the Library or the Storyline to the Viewscreen.

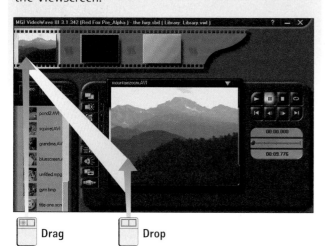

Drag   Drop

8 Add the Other Title

Click the **Text Animator** button and type the other part of the title that you want to appear in the scene. In this example, I typed the second line of my two-line header; this line will fly in from the bottom of the screen and meet up with the first line in the middle of the screen.

9 Set the Motion

Use the **Start**, **Hold**, and **Finish** buttons and the **Position** grid to set the motion for the text you just entered. Make sure that it complements the motion of the text in the color panel—the lines of text shouldn't run over each other, for instance.

10 Switch to the Video Animator

Click the **Video Animator** button to get ready to combine the two layers of this complex title scene.

Click

11 Add the Color Panel

Drag the named color panel with the other half of the title from the **Library** to the **Video Animator** screen. (The **Foreground** square in the console shows the color panel loaded.) Size the color panel to 100% in the **Start**, **Hold**, and **Finish** zones of the scene.

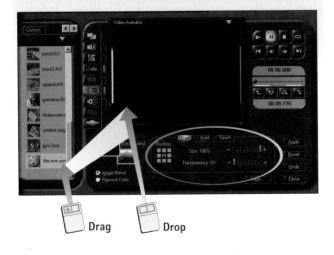

Drag   Drop

12 Remove the Color

Click the **Remove Color** option and select the black background of the color panel from the **Color** list. You should now be able to preview the titles moving around the scene. If you like the result, click the **Apply** button.

Click

End

How to Make Titles with Video in the Letters

Imagine a scene in which letters move across a plain-colored background; in the letters themselves, you see moving video. It's as if the letters were cut out of a mask, revealing the scene behind the mask. If that sounds like an effect you'd like to try, you're in luck—this task teaches you how to do it.

Large crawling title moves to the left.

"Transparent" font shows a moving video clip through the letters.

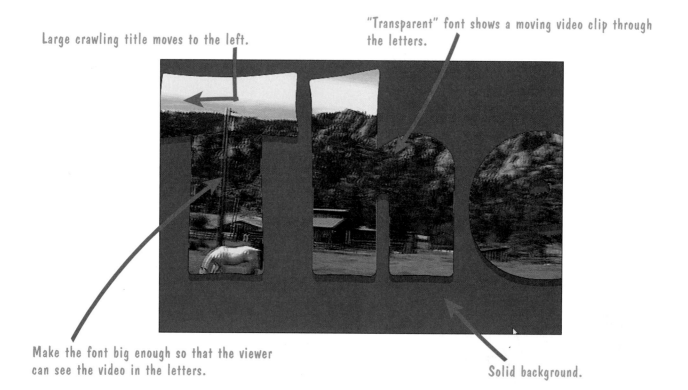

Make the font big enough so that the viewer can see the video in the letters.

Solid background.

Choose the Right Letters

This technique works well—if you're using the right font. Make sure that the letters are big and fat, not skinny. Use sans-serif fonts (simple letters that don't have tails and fancy legs at their bottoms). And make the letters as large as possible—cover the whole screen and move them across the display slowly so that the viewer can appreciate both what the text says and what the video is behind the letters.

1 Create a Color Panel

Start by creating a color panel; make it any color you want. (You might want to consider making it a color that will contrast nicely with the dominant colors of the video clip you will be using.)

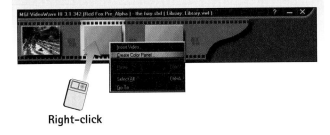

Right-click

2 Set the Duration

This panel must play as long as you want the title to appear. Decide on the video clip you want to "poke through" the letters and use the duration of that clip to help you determine the duration of the color panel. Then set the duration for which the color panel will run.

3 Switch to the Text Animator

Click the **Text Animator** button so that you can type the text that will appear on the color panel.

Click

4 Add the Titles

In the text box, type the text of the title. Click the **Font** button and choose a big, fat font; to see the video behind the color panel, you'll need a wide, bold font (such as Zurich, Verdana, Kristen, or Litho in bold and large enough to fill the screen, probably over 100 points). Click **OK**.

continues

5 Apply the Changes

When the title meets your satisfaction, click the **Apply** button to save the color panel and its text to the Storyline.

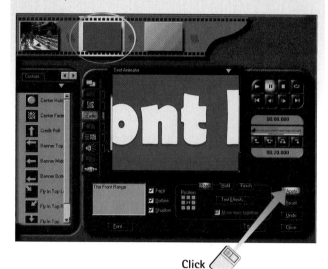

Click

6 Add Panel to the Library

To use the color panel and its text in the **Video Animator**, the panel must first exist in the Library. (Click the **Cutting Room** button if necessary to display the **Video** tab of the Library.) Drag it from the Storyline to the Library; when prompted by the **Save As** dialog box, give the panel a filename.

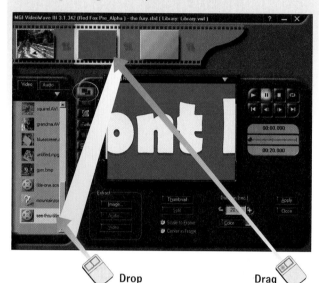

Drop   Drag

7 Add the Video Clip

Find the video clip you want to show through the letters in the title and drag it to the Viewscreen.

8 Open the Video Animator

Click the **Video Animator** button to begin the process of combining the video clip with the title on the color panel.

Click

9   Add the Color Panel

Drag the color panel with the title from the Library to the Video Animator. (The **Foreground** square shows when the color panel is loaded.) For each of the **Start**, **Hold**, and **Finish** zones, set the size of the panel to **100%**.

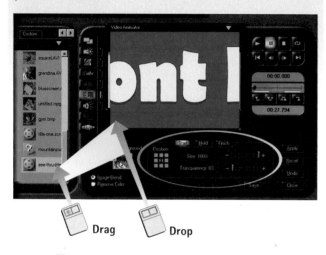

Drag   Drop

10   Remove the Color

Click the **Remove Color** button to set the animator to chroma key mode. In the next step, we actually tell VideoWave which color to remove from the color panel letters so that the video shows through the text.

Click

11   Choose the Text Color

Click the **Color** button next to the **Remove Color** option and click **Pick a Color**. Now position the eyedropper tool, in the Viewscreen itself, over the one of the letters in the title. Click to select the color of the letter (not the background color). Click **OK**.

Click

12   Set the Tolerance

Finally, bump up the **Tolerance** slider until the video shows through the letters for each of the Start, Hold, and Finish positions (you want the letters to stay transparent throughout the video). Preview the effect with the VCR controls and click **Apply** to save your changes.

End

Project 1

Creating a Complete Home Movie

Now you know enough about the video process to complete your own video. In this project, we go through all the steps for making a simple video complete with music, titles, and transitions.

Title panel. Scenes from the Library.

Transitions.

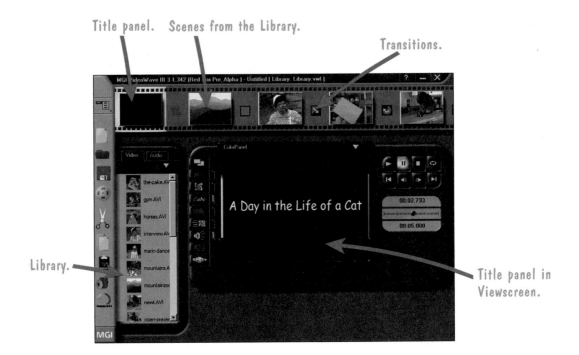

A Day in the Life of a Cat

Library.

Title panel in Viewscreen.

Getting Started with Video

When you sit down to make your first video, you can use this project as a general guide. But remember some of these rules. After you're comfortable with video production, experiment with breaking the rules!

- Keep your scenes short—no more than 4 minutes each.

- Mix long and short scenes.

- Use transitions sparingly—usually just cut from one scene to another.

- Start with titles, use captions occasionally, and end with rolling credits and music.

- Use music as a soundtrack.

1 Start Fresh

Clear the Storyline of any old clips that might be stored there by choosing **Storyline, New** from the menu button. If you need to, also delete clips you don't need from the Library.

Click

2 Capture Your Video

Assuming that you have a camcorder full of clips aching to be seen, click the **Capture** button and, with VideoWave configured for capturing, record video from tape. Repeat the capture process until all the clips have been stored in the Library.

3 Capture Other Audio

While you're in Capture mode, capture any audio (such as a song from CD) that you'll need for the video production.

4 Go to the Cutting Room

Click the **Cutting Room** button to exit from Capture mode and get ready for video assembly.

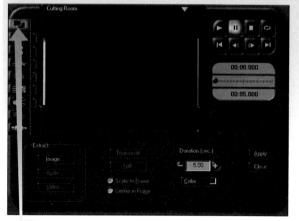

 Click

continues

5 Add the Clips

Drag the clips you want to use in your movie from the Library to the Storyline. Arrange them in the order you want your video to unfold.

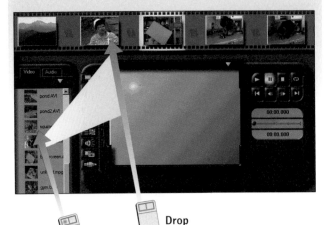

Drag

Drop

6 Create a Color Panel

Now we'll create the title screen. To do that, right-click a blank frame at the end of the video Storyline and choose **Create Color Panel** from the shortcut menu. From the **Color** drop-down list at the bottom of the Cutting Room console, select a color for your color panel.

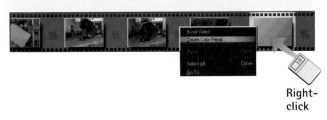

Right-click

7 Move the Panel

After you've created the color panel, drag it to the front of your Storyline and make it the new first frame of the video. Double-click the color panel frame in the Storyline to put it in the Viewscreen.

8 Go to the Text Animator

Click the **Text Animator** button to add titles for the video to the color panel you just created.

 Click

9 Add the Titles

Type the title of the video and select a font and a font size by clicking the **Font** button. Remember that titles should be fairly large (between 24 and 36 points is a good average).

Double-click

10 Animate the Title

If you want, use the **Paths** tab in the Library to animate the title with an effect such as **Fly In**. Double-click the text effect you want and then click the **Play** button in the VCR controls to observe the effect. Use the **Start**, **Hold**, and **Finish** buttons under the VCR controls to change the timing and the appearance.

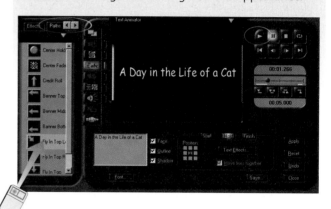

11 Go to the Audio Studio

You'll probably want the video to kick off with some music. With the title screen still in the Viewscreen, click the **Audio Studio** button.

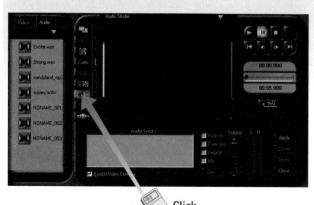

Click

12 Add Some Music

On the **Audio** tab in the Library, find the CD audio file you captured earlier in the project and drag it into the **Audio Tracks** box in the Audio Studio console. This song undoubtedly runs longer than the short title sequence and continues playing through the first scene or two of the film. Click the **Clip** button if you want to fade or trim the song.

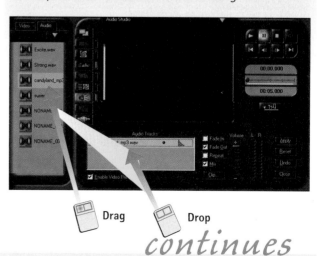

Drag   **Drop**

continues

Project 1: Creating a Complete Home Movie   135

Creating a Complete Home Movie Continued

13 Apply Your Changes

Click the **Apply** button to update the Storyline. Keep in mind that although you can preview your movie at any time, VideoWave won't show you all the pieces working together because that requires too much computer processing. You'll only see it all working as a complete film after you produce the movie.

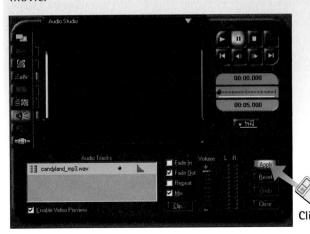

 Click

14 Add Transitions

Now we'll add a transition between the first two clips. In the Storyline, double-click the transition placeholder between the two scenes. Notice that you're in Transitions mode now.

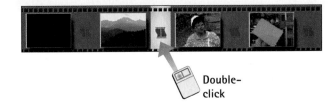

 Double-click

15 Add a Dissolve

Drag the **Dissolve** transition from the Library and drop it on the **Transitions** screen. Click the VCR **Play** button to observe the effect and then click **Apply** to add the effect to the Storyline.

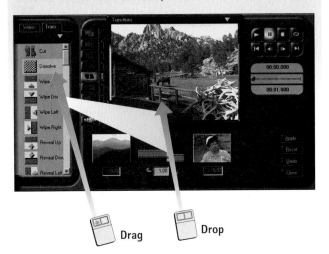

Drag   Drop

16 Make Other Transitions

Repeat Steps 14 and 15 to add transitions between other clips in the video. Remember the rule to use transitions sparingly; too many transitions make your movie look like an amateur transition showcase. I recommend that you pick a subtle transition and use it only occasionally.

17 Add a Color Panel

We're going to finish the video with a credit roll at the end of the video. Let's roll the credits over another color panel. (Alternatively, you could roll the credits over the last video clip.) Right-click a blank frame at the end of the video and choose **Create Color Panel** from the shortcut menu.

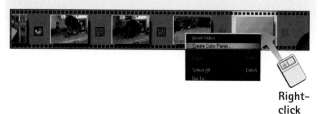

Right-click

18 Go to the Text Animator

Click the **Text Animator** button to get ready to add the credits for the video.

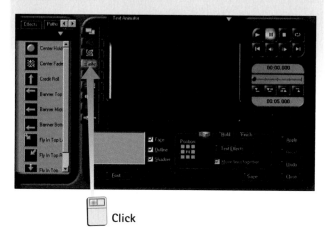

Click

19 Type the Credits

Type the credits into the text box. Use a hard return between lines and use three dots to separate names from titles. Click the **Font** button to choose a font and type size for the credit text; remember that credit text is not as large as the title text you created earlier (14 or 16 points is generally good for credits).

20 Choose the Credit Roll

Drag the **Credit Roll** effect from the **Paths** tab of the Library and drop it to the Text Animator. Click the **Apply** button to save the changes. To preview the entire movie, Shift-select all the scenes in the Storyline and then click the **Play** button in the VCR controls. Remember that the preview might look a little choppy—especially around transitions. It will also be missing any additional music tracks you may have applied. When you finally produce the movie, all the elements will be in place and play flawlessly.

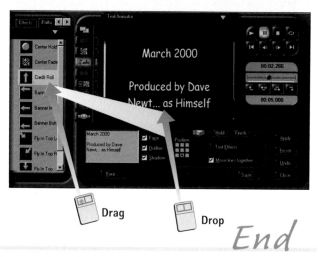

Drag   Drop

End

Task

PART 6

Working with Audio

*I*n the world of video, the visuals tell only half the story. Less than half the story, if you believe sound engineers. In reality, the *audio*—narration, music, even *Foley effects* (special sound effects for creaking doors, gunshots, and car engines, for instance) if you're really fancy—fills in the gaps and turns your simple video clips into a sophisticated multimedia presentation.

For most of us, 90% of the sound in a home movie comes straight from your camcorder, recorded along with the video at the time you were shooting. Sure, you can add sound effects after the principal photography is over, but I'm guessing you don't have the time or patience for that. Instead, the tasks in this part of the book show you how to add music and other sound effects to the audio you already have, creating a cohesive audio-video product. By using a program such as VideoWave, you can easily capture music from the Internet (in the form of MP3 files) or from audio CDs and apply it to the background of your videos as music soundtracks. ●

How to Capture a Song from CD

VideoWave makes it easy to capture music from an audio CD and incorporate it into a movie in Windows' common WAV format. In fact, you can use VideoWave to capture CD audio that you want to use in Premiere—the format will be the same.

The Library lists audio tracks as well as video clips.

The same button starts and stops recording.

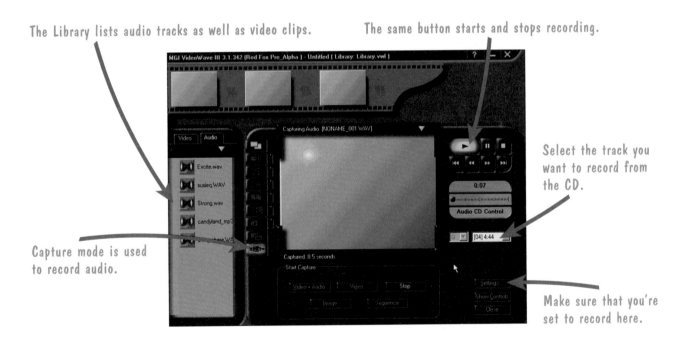

Select the track you want to record from the CD.

Capture mode is used to record audio.

Make sure that you're set to record here.

Beware of Copyrights

I could write an entire chapter about copyright, and in fact I have—I deal with copyright laws for photographic images in another book, *Digital Photography Answers* (published by Osborne McGraw-Hill). The key thing to remember about copyright is this:

You can copy commercial music only for your own personal use. If you're making a student film that might see general exhibition, you must obtain permission from the publisher to capture and play back music, even if you own the CD.

1 Go to Capture

Click the **Capture** button to switch to VideoWave's **Capture** mode. In addition to recording video from your camcorder, this mode enables you to record audio from your PC's CD player.

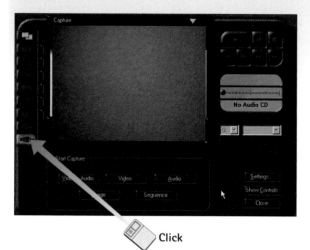

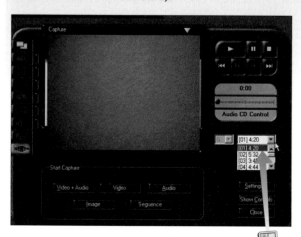
Click

2 Verify Your Settings

Click the **Settings** button in the lower-right corner of the console area. The **Capture Settings** dialog box opens. In the **Audio** section, make sure that the **Capture Device** option lists your sound card, not the video capture hardware. Also make sure that you select **Auto-Start CD During Capture**. Then click the **Audio Mixing** button to open the **Audio Input Mixing** dialog box. Make sure that the **Compact Disc Balance** option is selected. Click OK twice to close both dialog boxes.

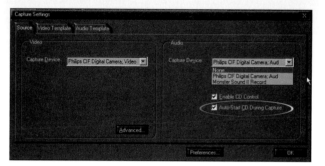

3 Choose the Track

Make sure that the CD you want to record from is in your PC's CD-ROM drive. From the drop-down list, choose the number of the CD track you want to record. You can also use the VCR controls to select the track you want. When you're ready to record, make sure that the audio is stopped (click the **Stop** button on the VCR controls).

4 Record the Song

Click the **Audio** button. The selected song will start playing and be recorded to the hard disk. When the song is over, click the **Stop** button. You will find the track with the label **NONAME** in the **Audio** tab of the Library; you can rename the file to anything you like.

Click

End

How to Capture a Song from CD   141

How to Capture Narration

One of the most useful kinds of audio you can add to a video is *narration*. A voiceover can add tremendous value to a video by explaining the situation to viewers. You can do the narration on-scene when you film the video, but you'll generally get better results by recording the voiceover in a quiet studio (such as at your PC) and adding it to the video afterwards.

Use the best mike you can afford.

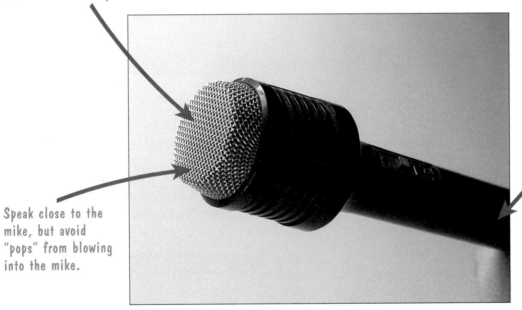

Record narrations and voiceovers "in studio" instead of on location with the camcorder.

Speak close to the mike, but avoid "pops" from blowing into the mike.

Tips for Better Audio

Voiceovers are often an afterthought, but with a little planning, you can get excellent results that really enhance the quality of your video:

- Use a quality microphone. The $5 mike that came with your PC simply isn't up to the task of recording quality audio.

- Get to know the mike. Speak at the proper distance from the mike so that the sound level is good without "popping" your audio and causing annoying audio glitches.

- Write a script. Don't narrate off the cuff. Write down the script and practice it, ideally in front of a running preview of the film.

1 Go to Capture

Click the **Capture** button to switch to VideoWave's **Capture** mode. This is the mode in which you record live audio.

Click

2 Verify Your Settings

Click the **Settings** button to open the **Capture Settings** dialog box. In the **Audio** section, make sure that the **Capture Device** option lists the device that controls your microphone (probably your sound card). Make sure that the **Auto-Start CD During Capture** option is not selected. Then click the **Audio Mixing** button to open the **Audio Input Mixing** dialog box. Make sure that the **Microphone Balance** option is selected. Click **OK** twice to close both dialog boxes.

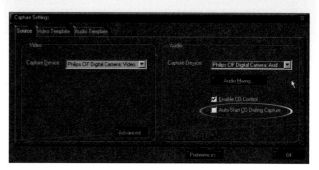

3 Start Recording

When you're ready to begin, click the **Audio** button and start reading your narration. Make sure that you enunciate clearly, speaking at the proper distance from the microphone to avoid unpleasant "pops" from certain letters you pronounce.

4 End Recording

When you're done recording the narration, click the **Stop** button to close the audio file and finish the recording. You will find the track with the label **NONAME** in the **Audio** tab of the Library; you can rename the file to anything you like.

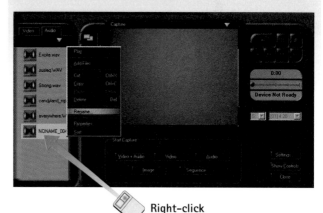

Right-click

End

How to Create
Background Music

Neither VideoWave nor Premiere has a way to create background music for your video. For that, you must have some musical skill and have access to some instruments—or use a music-authoring program. I like Cambium's Sound Choice, a program with a large selection of soundtrack-quality clips in a variety of styles. Here's how to create some background music in a program such as Sound Choice and then import the sound file into VideoWave.

Use multimedia software to create original music.

Audio clips you've recorded or imported are in the Library.

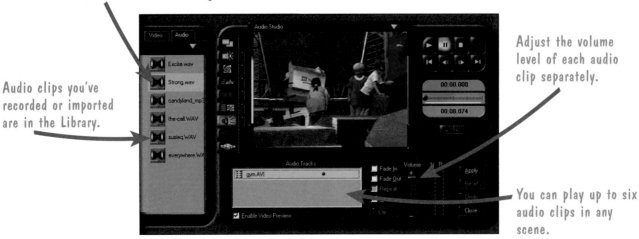

Adjust the volume level of each audio clip separately.

You can play up to six audio clips in any scene.

Why Use Music Software?

Why bother using music-authoring software such as Sound Choice when you can just copy a few tracks from your favorite CD? As mentioned earlier, copyright laws can bite you if you're not careful. Multimedia-authoring software that burns audio tracks for you is designed to be royalty free. That means you can use it in a movie and not worry about having the rights to use it. But watch out for the fine print—some software limits how you can use the music that it generates.

Roll Your Own

If you want to create your own original music, you can do that, too. It helps to have some good recording equipment, such as some high-quality mikes and perhaps a 4-track recording deck to produce your music. You can capture the completed song into VideoWave by connecting the deck with the music to your PC's line-in sound port and use the procedure outlined in Task 1, "How to Capture a Song from CD."

1 Find a Song

Sound Choice, like most multimedia-authoring software, has a library of prerecorded tunes. Surf around the songs and find one that you like. You can also search through the songs by keyword, so you can look for songs that have a specific theme, evoke a particular emotion, or have certain instruments in them.

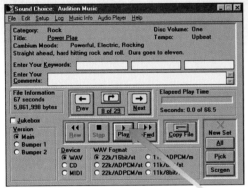

Click

2 Choose a Length

Sound Choice includes several versions of each song in a variety of lengths. Choose the length you need based on how long the scene is that you want to enhance with music. Shorter clips are referred to as "bumps" (hence **Bumper**), and longer versions are labeled **Main**. When you select a version, the length appears in the **File Information** part of the screen.

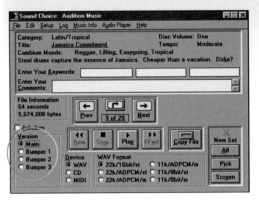

3 Copy the Clip

Click the **Copy File** button. In the **Copy Music** dialog box that opens, you can shorten the clip using the **Copy Shortened File** button, or you can just click the **Copy Full File** button. If necessary, change the location on the hard disk where the file will be saved and click **Save**.

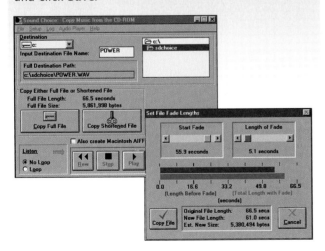

4 Import Audio File into VideoWave

Back in VideoWave, click the list menu arrow in the Library and choose **Add Files**. Locate the file you just created and select it. The file should now appear in the **Audio** tab of the Library, ready for your use in VideoWave.

Click

End

How to Mix Audio Tracks

The preceding few tasks have shown you how to create and import audio tracks into your video editor but haven't really shown you how to use those files. Well, fret no more; this task shows you how to load some audio tracks into VideoWave and Premiere.

Although Premiere lets you use up to 99 simultaneous audio and video tracks, VideoWave is a bit more limited—you can add a total of only 6 audio tracks to a single scene. Usually, however, that's plenty.

Audio being previewed in the **Source Monitor** window.

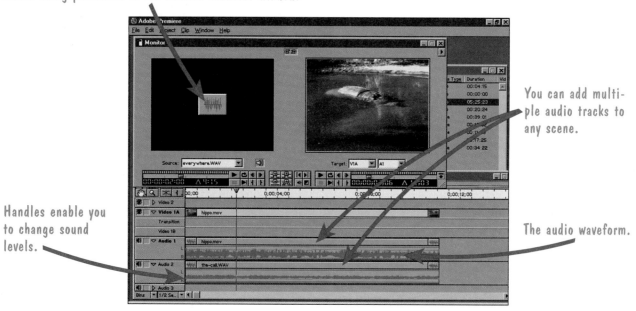

You can add multiple audio tracks to any scene.

Handles enable you to change sound levels.

The audio waveform.

Audio Formats

Audio on the PC has changed a lot in the past few years. The changes have come about because lots of people are downloading songs from the Internet and listening to music on their computers. Here's what you should know about sound formats:

- **WAV.** The WAV format is quite old. All video editors work with this format, which is **lossless**—that is, there's no compression to degrade sound quality.

- **CD-Audio.** Audio CDs use a high-quality sound format that can be read and converted to other computer formats. VideoWave can read audio CDs, although Premiere cannot.

- **MP3.** The MP3 format compresses sound files to save disk space and download time, but does so without losing the CD quality of the sound. MP3 is extremely popular on the Internet. You can also use special software to turn a CD-Audio file into an MP3 file. VideoWave reads MP3 files but Premiere does not.

1   Add the Video V

Load a video clip into the Viewscreen. This is the clip to which you will add a second audio track. (The first audio track is the one you recorded when you filmed the video originally.)

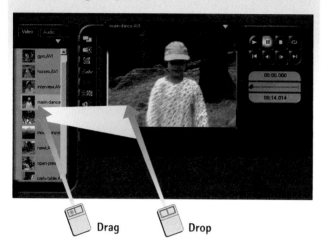

Drag   Drop

2   Preview Audio Files V

If you want to hear a sound clip, click the **Audio** tab in the Library and then right-click a clip in the list that appears. Choose **Play** from the menu. Right-click and choose **Stop** to end the playback. (Note that you can't preview music if you're already in the Audio Studio; to preview music, click another of the Mode Selector buttons to go to some other part of the program.)

Right-click

3   Go to the Audio Studio V

Click the **Audio Studio** button to edit the sound in the scene. You should see a suite of audio tools appear in the console.

Click

4   Add a Sound Clip V

From the **Audio** tab of the Library, drag a sound clip to the Viewscreen. Note that the sound clip's file-name appears in the **Audio Tracks** list under the Viewscreen. It's important to realize that if you add a clip that's longer than the scene, the clip will continue playing into the next scene.

Drag   Drop

continues

5 Select a Level V

You can adjust the level of each audio track independently so that one is louder than the other is. From the **Audio Track** list, select the audio track you just added and adjust the volume level by using the **Volume** slider. Do the same for the track's primary audio track. Test the results using the VCR controls. VideoWave doesn't let you fade one clip into another; for more precise control over multiple audio tracks, you need to use Premiere.

6 Apply the Audio V

You can add as many as five additional audio tracks to the scene if you want. When you're happy with the audio you've added, click the **Apply** button to update the scene in the Storyline.

Click

1 Add Clips to the Project P

Before you can begin using audio in Premiere, you must add at least one audio clip to the **Project** window. Do it the same way you add video: right-click a blank area in the window and choose **Import, File** from the shortcut menu. Unlike VideoWave, which can read MP3 files, Premiere can understand only the WAV audio format.

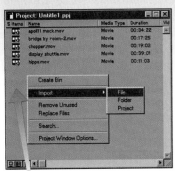

Right-click

2 Put Audio in Source Monitor P

Assuming that you want to preview an audio clip before you insert it in the project, double-click the filename in the **Project** window. The file should appear in the **Source Monitor** window.

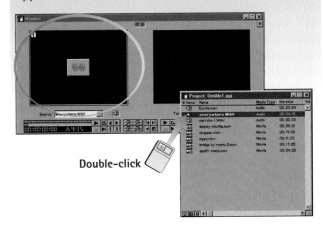

Double-click

3 Preview the Audio P

To listen to the clip, click the **Play** button in the **Monitor** window. Click the **Stop** button to stop the playback of the audio file.

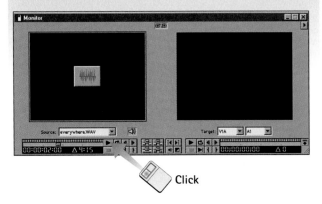

Click

4 Add the Audio P

Now add the sound clip to the **Timeline**. Assuming that there's already a video clip in **Video 1A** (and if there isn't, add one now), you should see its audio component in the **Audio 1** track. Drag the audio clip you just auditioned to the **Audio 2** track.

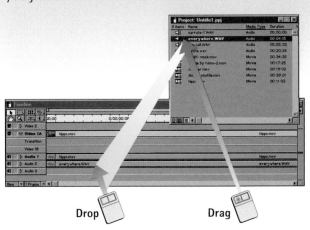

Drop   Drag

5 View the Wave P

Now adjust the relative volume of the two audio tracks. Start by clicking the right-facing arrows next to the **Audio 1** and **Audio 2** tracks in the **Timeline** window. The tracks should expand to display the waveforms of the two sound files.

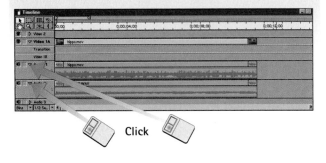

Click

6 Change the Level P

You should see a red line that runs through the middle of both waveforms. Grab a line by the handle on the left side of the window and drag it down to lower the volume. Drag the right handle down to keep the line horizontal to reduce the volume of the entire clip.

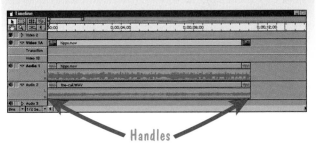

Handles

End

How to Fade Audio

In the last task, you learned how to mix a second (or third) audio track into a scene, as well as to vary the volumes of the sound tracks. Although this is a great technique to implement, even more frequently you'll want to fade the music in at the beginning of the scene or fade it out at the end. As you're about to see, VideoWave makes it easy to do a simple fade; Premiere gives you the power to vary the volume many times throughout the scene.

Both audio tracks play during this clip.

Add handles to vary the volume at any point.

Audio ramps up.

Audio fades down.

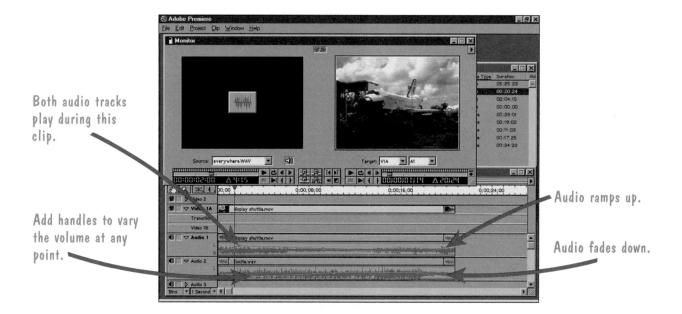

When to Fade

Why fade the audio to begin with? There are many reasons to fade, but here are a few to get you started:

- To end music that's longer than the scene
- To introduce music slowly into a scene
- To slowly ramp up the volume of dialog in a scene while reducing the volume of the background music (or vice versa)

1 Open the Audio Studio V

Load the scene you want to work with in the Viewscreen and then click the **Audio Studio** button. If you don't already have your second audio track loaded, drag it to the Viewscreen now.

Click

2 Apply Fade Controls V

Click one of the audio tracks in the **Audio Tracks** list. Then place checkmarks in the **Fade In** and **Fade Out** boxes to tell VideoWave to fade this sound file in and out of the scene. (You can also select just one or the other of these options.) Click another audio track in the scene and apply the desired fade to that one. Click the **Apply** button to save your changes.

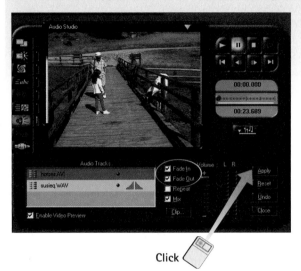

Click

1 Create Handles P

Premiere doesn't have a one-click fade control; instead, you can raise and lower the volume of a sound clip many times through the scene. Load the video clip and the additional sound clip files in Premiere as usual. In the **Timeline**, you should see the waveform for your audio track (if not, click the right arrow next to the desired audio track to expand the display). The waveform already has a volume handle at each end; add two more handles by clicking the red line at two places in the track.

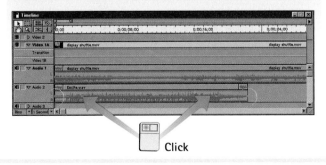

Click

2 Drag the Handles P

Drag the handles to create a fade. For example, drag the new handles so that the volume goes up for most of the clip and then goes back down again. You can add more handles and drag them around to create sophisticated audio control of your scene.

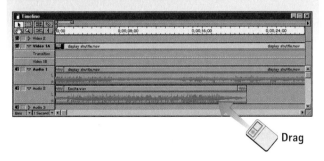

Drag

End

How to Trim Audio

The audio files you create for your movies won't always be exactly the right length. Sometimes, the sound clip is too long, and you'll want to modify the video to fix the problem (as described in the next task); other times, you'll want to trim the length of the audio file itself. Perhaps the sound clip has ugly mike pops at the start or end. This task shows you how to trim VideoWave audio. (In Premiere, you trim audio in the **Monitor** window, exactly as you trim video.)

Top blue bar: Scene length.
Bottom white bar: Audio length.

Audio clip length.

Mark-Out audio.

Mark-In audio.

Video clip length.

Second audio clip.

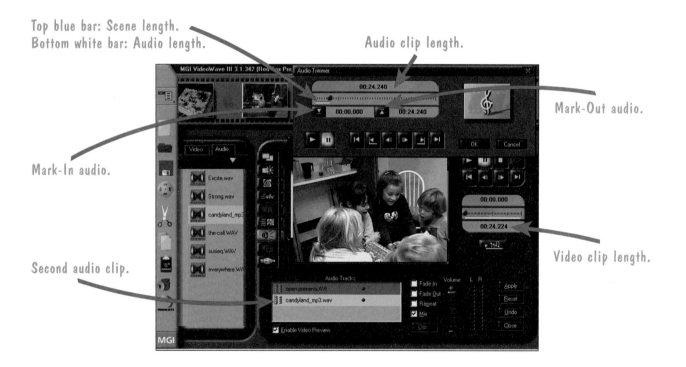

Audio That Spans Scenes

A long audio clip can run longer than a single scene in VideoWave. For proof, click the **Clip** button in the **Audio Studio** console to display the **Audio Trimmer** dialog box. An audio track that is longer than the video keeps playing into the next scene unless you clip it to stop sooner. When you preview the clip all by itself, the audio stops when the video stops. You have to preview multiple scenes to hear the entire clip. For more precise control over these kinds of audio situations, however, switch to Premiere.

1 Go to the Audio Studio

Load a video clip in the Viewscreen and click the **Audio Studio** button.

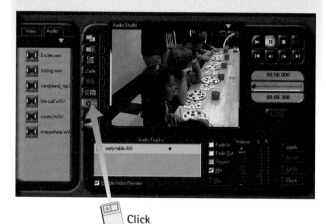

Click

2 Load the Audio Clip

If your video clip doesn't already have a second audio clip associated with it, add a second sound clip to the video by dragging the file from the **Audio** tab in the Library now.

Drag   Drop

3 Open the Audio Trimmer

Select the new clip in the **Audio Tracks** list and click the **Clip** button. The **Audio Trimmer** dialog box opens. Note that you can't trim the length of the first audio track (the one that is part of the video).

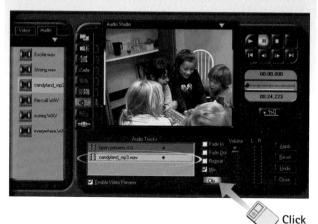

Click

4 Mark the Start and End

The **Audio Trimmer** dialog box enables you to play the audio and set the Mark-In and Mark-Out points—in other words, the points in the song where it begins to play and where it stops playing. This is handy if you want only a short section of the middle of a song to play in the scene. Use the **Play** button or the slider to set the location, and then click the **Mark-In Point** when you want the clip to begin playing. Then find the point where you want the song to stop playing and click the **Mark-Out Point**. Click **OK** to complete the process.

White audio file line is much longer than blue video file line.

End

TASK 7

How to Extend Video to Match Audio

Sometimes, your audio track is longer than the video intended to run behind it. You might run into this situation with a background song that runs a little long or a narrator who talks a little too slowly. Whatever the case, you can add more video to fill in the hole, trim the audio short (as explained in the preceding task), or add extra frames to the end of the scene so that a *freeze frame* runs while the audio ends.

The audio file is longer than the video scene.

The last frame of the video "holds" the scene while the audio plays.

Don't use this technique for more than a few seconds.

Point of transition to freeze frame.

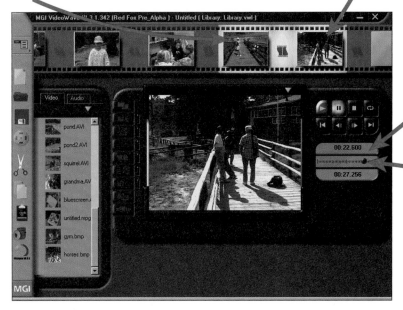

How Much Quality Do You Need?

When you record audio, you have a lot of choices for audio quality. VideoWave reduces what could be dozens of options down to just three. Here's when to use each one:

- **AM Radio Quality.** This is 11KHz, 8-bit stereo. It's very low quality and should only be used for recording voice. Even then, I'd avoid using it.

- **FM Radio Quality.** This is 22KHz, 16-bit stereo. It's much better than AM Radio Quality and is good for most home-brewed videos. Use this option for voice and sound effects.

- **CD Quality.** This 44KHz, 16-bit stereo is most appropriate for music. Using this option for voice recordings is probably overkill.

1 Go to the Audio Studio V

Load the scene that has the too-long audio into the Viewscreen. Then click the **Audio Studio** button.

Click

2 Determine the Total Length V

If the audio clip isn't already attached to the clip, include it now. Select the too-long audio clip and click the **Clip** button to open the **Audio Trimmer** dialog box. Note the total audio length and click the **Cancel** button.

3 Apply Your Changes V

If you haven't already saved the video clip with the second audio track, click the **Apply** button now.

Click

4 Go to the Cutting Room V

Click the **Cutting Room** button so that you can extract the end of the scene as a still frame.

Click

continues

5 Scroll to the End

In the pane under the VCR controls, drag the brown circle to the very end of the slider to move directly to the end of the video clip.

Drag

6 Extract the Last Frame

With the Viewscreen showing the last frame of the scene, click the **Image** button in the **Extract** section of the **Cutting Room** console. The **Extract Images** dialog box opens.

 Click

7 Add to Storyline

Select the **Add to Storyline** checkbox and click the **Extract** button to make a copy of this last frame of video and save it as a bitmapped image. Then click the **Close** button to close the dialog box.

Click

8 Display the Frame

Locate the saved frame at the end of the Storyline. Drag it from there to the Viewscreen so that you can edit it.

Drop Drag

9 Go to the Cutting Room **V**

Click the **Cutting Room** button so that you can work on the still image in the Cutting Room. You want to adjust the length of the image so that it perfectly fills in the space between the time that the video would otherwise have ended and when the audio track ends.

Click

11 Apply Your Changes **V**

Click the **Apply** button. The scene now holds on the last frame for as long as the audio continues to play.

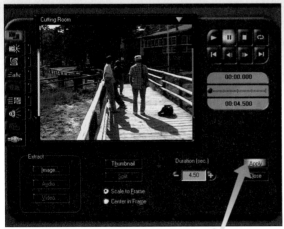

Click

10 Change the Duration **V**

Set the **Duration** box for the frame so that the frame remains onscreen long enough to fill in for the over-long audio. You need to subtract the duration of the original video scene from the total length of the audio to determine how long this freeze frame will remain onscreen.

1 Extract the Last Frame **P**

The procedure to freeze a frame in Premiere is essentially the same as it is in VideoWave, but you have to know how to grab that last frame. Display the scene in the **Monitor** window and go to the end of the clip. Choose **File, Export, Frame** from the menu and save the frame as a BMP file to your hard disk. You can then load the frame file into the **Project** window and stretch it appropriately in the **Timeline**.

End

How to Create an Audio Transition

It's a common technique—so common, in fact, that you might not even notice it is happening. Filmmakers like to transition to new scenes aurally, not visually. Often, you can hear the next scene—such as a person's voice, street traffic, or a telephone—a few seconds before you see it happen onscreen. Then the scene changes, and the audio is perfectly in synch with the visuals. You can't do this in VideoWave, but you can in Premiere. Here's how.

Second scene.

First scene.

Video 2 "hides" Video 1A.

Videos overlap by few seconds.

The viewer hears the roller coaster screams before the next scene actually starts.

Getting the Most Out of Audio Transitions

Audio transitions are more popular than video transitions in most movies. Here are some tips to remember when you create your transitions:

- Keep them short. Don't play more than just a few short seconds of audio or the magic of the transition is lost.

- Don't combine an audio transition with any kind of video transition—just use a simple cut.

- Fade the outgoing audio. However, don't be too obvious about dropping out the audio from the first scene or the effect will be ruined.

- Use audio transitions on scenes in which you can cut to the next scene at a dramatic moment or use a subtle effect (such as a ringing phone) to signal the scene change.

1 Add the First Scene **P**

For this technique to work, we take advantage of Premiere's video layers: Higher track numbers obscure tracks with lower numbers. Drag the first scene from the **Monitor** window or the **Project** window to track **Video 2** in the **Timeline** window.

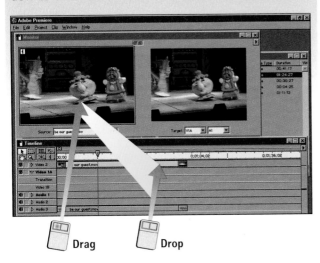

Drag   Drop

2 Add the Second Scene **P**

Drag the second video scene from the **Monitor** window or the **Project** window to the **Video 1A** track in the **Timeline**.

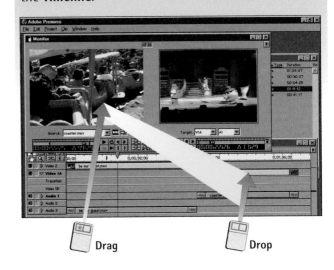

Drag   Drop

3 Set the Timing **P**

In the **Timeline**, drag the clip in **Video 1A** track back a little so that it starts before the clip in the **Video 2** track ends. Back it just up a few seconds at most.

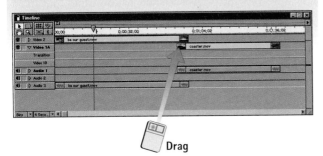

Drag

4 Fade the First Scene **P**

If you want, you can fade the audio at the end of the first scene a little to emphasize the audio that plays from the second scene. When you play these clips, you hear the action in the second scene before you see it. A flair for the dramatic can help you know when to make the cut.

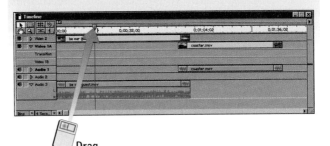

Drag

End

Task

PART 7

Working with Still Images

One of the great things about digital video is that still images and moving video are so closely related. Not only can you extract stills from a video clip, you can also include still images in your movie in a sort of video slideshow. Equipped with just a camcorder, you can make both video and still shots that you can print and email.

Don't be fooled by the marketing hype, either—no matter what kind of digital camcorder you own, you can extract still images from video. Of course, some cameras give you a little more flexibility. Some JVC and Sony cameras, for instance, enable you to take stills and copy the pictures to a removable memory card.

Nonetheless, the ability to pull a still out of video is a great feature. You can shoot continuous video and then grab the one moment that's "perfect" as a still. Or you can grab lots of stills and make a video slideshow out of them, complete with background music. (I explain how to do that in detail in Project 2.)

Interested in the potential of still images? Great. In the tasks in this part, I'll show you how to capture stills from video, edit them in a simple image editor such as Paint Shop Pro, and use them in video. ●

How to Capture an Image from Video

Unlike analog video you'd get with an ordinary camcorder, digital video can make good still frames that you can extract and print, email, or include in other documents. You can even reuse the still in the video, as you'll see later in the book.

You can include stills in your video project.

Use the Cutting Room to grab and edit stills.

The duration of the still.

A still image grabbed from a video clip or imported from a digital camera.

The Library holds the still images.

Good Freeze Frames Aren't Easy

Considering the nature of video, every freeze-frame image isn't going to be exactly frozen. Especially with analog video, you can get a lot of noise, blur, and even a mixture of two different images in alternating lines. Jagged edges might also be apparent. If your video capture device has controls for smoothing out extracted images, experiment with them. If not, you can try grabbing the still just a little sooner or a little later on the tape, where the artifacts might be less apparent.

By jogging the tape around, you can find the optimum point at which to grab the still.

1 Load the Video V

Find the clip from which you want to extract a still image and drag it to the Viewscreen.

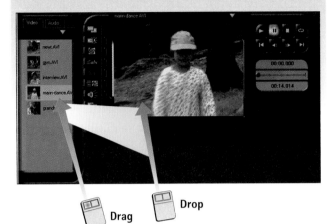

Drag **Drop**

2 Go to the Cutting Room V

Click the **Cutting Room** button. The Cutting Room controls appear in the console area.

Click

3 Find the Frame V

Using the VCR slider, find the moment in the video clip that you want to capture.

4 Start the Extraction V

In the **Extract** area of the Cutting Room console, click the **Image** button. The **Extract Images** dialog box appears.

continues

How to Capture an Image from Video Continued

5 Set the Save Location V

Where do you want to save this image? Click the **Browse** button and specify a filename and a location on your hard drive where you want to save the image you are going to extract.

6 Add to Storyline V

If you want this image to appear in the Storyline, click the **Add to Storyline** checkbox. Otherwise, leave it blank. You can always add the still to the movie later.

7 Extract the Image V

Click the **Extract** button. After a few seconds, the image is saved to your hard disk. You can work with it just as you would any graphic.

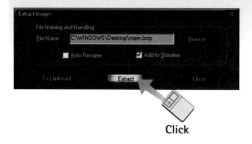

Click

8 Close the Dialog Box V

The **Extract Images** dialog box won't close on its own—it stays open in case you want to extract more still images. Click the **Close** button to return to the Cutting Room.

1 Load the Video **P**

In Premiere, the process of creating a still image is actually simpler than it is in VideoWave. Start by dragging a clip from the **Project** window to the **Source Monitor** window.

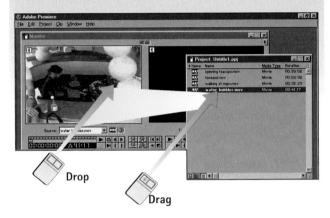

Drop

Drag

2 Find the Frame **P**

Use the slider in the Source **Monitor** window to find the point in the video clip that you want to capture.

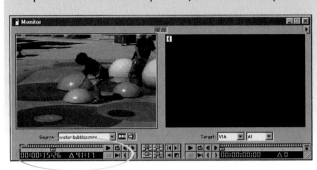

3 Extract the Image **P**

Choose **File, Export, Frame** from the menu. The **Export Still Frame** dialog box appears.

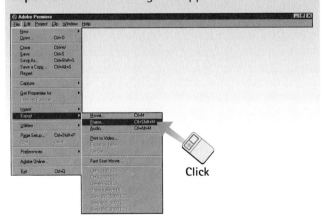

Click

4 Save the File **P**

By default, the still image is saved in the BMP file format. If you want to use another format, click the **Settings** button and make the change. Otherwise, simply name the file, choose a location on the hard drive where you want to store the file, and click the **Save** button.

Click

End

How to Change Image Resolution

The *resolution* of an image, measured in *pixels*, represents both the overall file size and the physical size at which the image will print. Images extracted from digital video are usually 720×480 pixels. Although this is a somewhat low resolution for a photograph (a 5×7-inch print, for instance, typically is about 1280×960 pixels—8×10s are even bigger), the resolution for the still image might be greater

(and the resulting file size bigger) than what you need. If you want to post the image to a Web page, for instance, you might want to shrink the image further. To do that, you should use an image editor. I prefer Jasc's Paint Shop Pro. Any image editor will do—you might already have Adobe PhotoShop or Corel Photo Paint, for instance—but I prefer the simplicity of Paint Shop Pro.

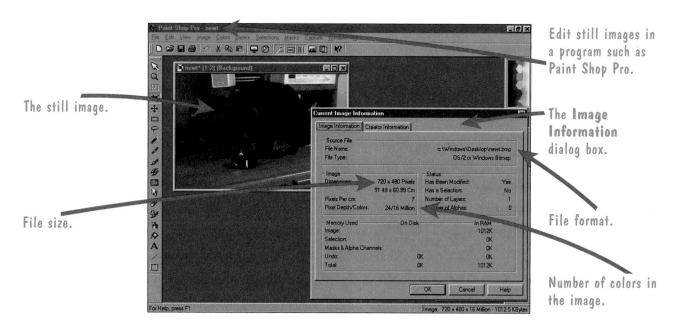

Edit still images in a program such as Paint Shop Pro.

The still image.

The **Image Information** dialog box.

File size.

File format.

Number of colors in the image.

Resolution Explained

It's important to understand the term *resolution* when you work with graphics. Resolution is the density of the pixels in an image. Digital video cameras capture images at a resolution of 720×480, which means 720 pixels in a line by 480 lines. At that resolution, you can't really print the image any bigger than 5×7 inches, but it's great for Web pages and importing into Word or Publisher documents.

If you want to print images and frame them on your wall, you need a digital camera that can grab images at a much higher resolution. These mega-pixel cameras take pictures with at least a million pixels in the image, such as 1280×960. Although a few digital camcorders can take high-resolution stills like this, you should look into one of the many megapixel still digital cameras if you want to take pictures for printing and framing.

1 Load the Image

In an image editor application such as Paint Shop Pro, open the image file you extracted from a video clip by using the **File, Open** menu option.

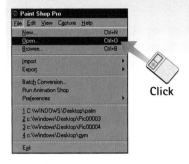

Click

2 Crop the Image

If you want to make the image smaller by trimming away unwanted details, click the **Crop** tool in the toolbar. Then click in the image area and drag to frame the portion of the image you want to keep. Click the **Crop Image** button in the **Controls** window.

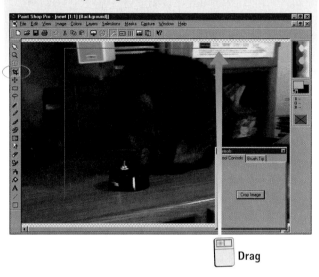

 Drag

3 Set a New Size

You can also shrink the image to a specific pixel size to drop the resolution. If you plan to insert this image in a Web page, for instance, you might want to choose a width of 400 pixels—a size at which the image will fit on the screen with enough room to spare in which you can put some text on the side. Choose **Image, Resize** from the menu. In the **Resize** dialog box, enter a new width or height in the **Pixel Size** area and click **OK**. Make sure that the **Maintain aspect ratio** box is selected so that you don't distort the image.

4 Save the Image

When you're done adjusting the image and its resolution, choose **File, Save As** from the menu to save the image on your hard drive. Note that you might want to give the modified image a different filename than the original image.

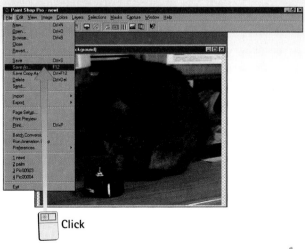

 Click

End

How to Change File Format

TASK 3

In a perfect world, there would be one universal file format for everything. Unfortunately, that's not the case. Your video editor might extract an image in BMP format, but you might have to convert it to the JPG or GIF format to make use of it. Converting the format of an image is a snap with an image editor program such as Paint Shop Pro.

The Crop tool makes the image smaller by discarding extra information.

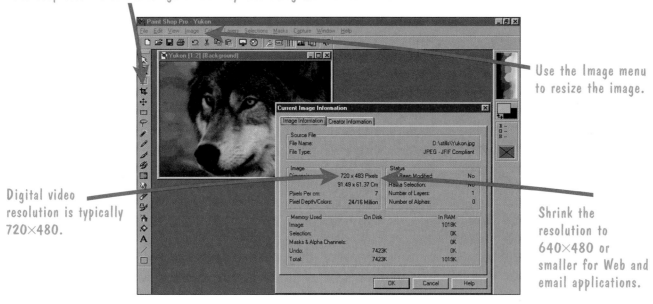

Use the Image menu to resize the image.

Digital video resolution is typically 720×480.

Shrink the resolution to 640×480 or smaller for Web and email applications.

Image File Formats

Here is what file formats are most commonly used for:

JPG. The JPG format is great for squeezing huge photographic images down to tiny file sizes while sacrificing only a little image quality. JPG is great for Web pages and email.

GIF. Commonly used in Web pages, GIF files can be made to display first in low resolution and then improve in quality as more data is downloaded.

TIF. This is a great format for preserving all the image quality in a picture, although files can be huge.

BMP. Used by Windows to display "wallpaper" images, it isn't practical for most other applications because of the large file sizes associated with the format.

1 Load the Image

In an image editor application such as Paint Shop Pro, open the image file you extracted from a video clip by using the **File, Open** menu. Recall that images extracted from video clips are typically in the BMP format.

2 Open the Save Dialog Box

Choose **File, Save As** from the menu. From the **Save as type** list, choose the format you want. The most common formats are JPG, BMP, GIF, PCX, and TIF. Name the file and click the **Save** button.

Click

3 Set the Format Options

Sometimes, you might encounter a dialog box that says you're about to save the image in fewer colors—perhaps even as few as two colors. If you see this dialog box, click **No** to close the warning box without saving the file. Back in the **Save As** dialog box, click the **Options** button.

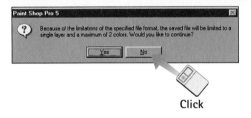

Click

4 Change the Version

In the **Save Options** dialog box that opens, set the file format to the latest version. The PCX file format, for instance, should be set to **Version 5** if you want to save lots of colors.

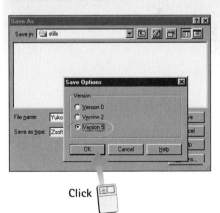

Click

End

How to Erase Parts of an Image

After you've extracted an image from a video clip, you can edit the image to your heart's content. One common problem with images culled from video is the presence of junk—such as telephone poles or other obstacles—that gets in the way of your main image. You can airbrush such objects out of the image using an image editor program such as Paint Shop Pro.

Editing is obvious if you look carefully.

We want to remove this tree from the image.

The tree is gone.

The tree was painted out by covering it with nearby background colors.

Cloning Tips

The **Clone Brush** in Paint Shop Pro is a great way to wipe out distracting parts of an image. You need to practice, though, to avoid smearing the background. Get in the habit of dabbing the brush on the screen. You can also vary the thickness of the brush tip to get a better erasure effect.

1 Load the Image

In an image editor application such as Paint Shop Pro, open the image file you extracted from a video clip by using the **File, Open** menu.

2 Select the Clone Brush

Click the **Clone Brush** tool in the toolbar. This tool enables you to paint one part of the image with actual pixels from another part of the picture. We'll use it to eliminate an eyesore from the image.

Click

3 Select the Source Region

Move the **Clone Brush** over a background part of the scene that's near the element you want to remove. Right-click to select those pixels; they're the pixels the **Clone Brush** will paint with.

Right-click

4 Paint

Paint the obstacle out of the image by clicking the left mouse button. It helps to "dab" the brush and work slowly, clicking many times instead of making big, sweeping strokes.

Click

End

How to Print an Image

After you've extracted and edited an image, you might want to print it to send it to friends or family who do not have access to the Internet or email. Although the images you extract from a video clip are not detailed enough to print and frame, images taken by a two-megapixel digital camera can be impressive enough to hang on the wall.

Choose **File**, **Print** to open the **Print** dialog box.

You can print an image file from a graphics program such as Paint Shop Pro.

Use the right kind of paper.

Verify the settings for your printer.

File Sizes and Printing

When you print an image, it will come out jagged and "pixely" unless the resolution of the file is sufficient for the size you want to print. Use this chart as a rule of thumb for sizing the images you want to print:

File Resolution	Maximum Print Size
640×480	5×7 inches
1 million pixels	8×10 inches
2 million pixels	11×17 inches

When printing on an inkjet printer, remember that the image quality greatly depends on the kind of paper you use. You get dramatically better results if you use glossy photo paper, available at any computer or office supply store.

1 Load the Image

Because there's no printing feature built into VideoWave, you need an image editor program such as Paint Shop Pro to print an image file. Using Paint Shop Pro's **File, Open** menu item, load the image.

2 Configure the Printer

Choose **File, Page Setup** to open the **Page Setup** dialog box; click the **Printer** button. From the **Name** drop-down list, choose the printer you plan to use. If you're using a color inkjet printer, click the **Properties** button and configure the printer to use the appropriate kind of paper.

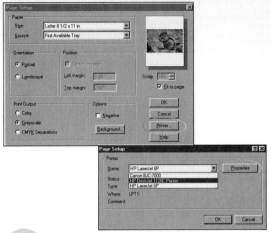

3 Orient the Print

After you close the **Printer Properties** dialog box, you should be back in the **Page Setup** dialog box. Select **Portrait** or **Landscape** orientation and then choose the scaling you want. (Scaling determines how large the image appears on the printed page.) If you choose **Fit to page**, the image will print at the full size of the paper. Click **OK** to close the dialog box.

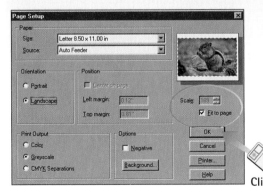

Click

4 Print

Choose **File, Print** from the menu to print the image. When the **Print** dialog box opens, check all the settings you have already made and then click the **OK** button.

Click

End

How to Email an Image

In the previous task, I showed you how to print an image. But emailing images is more efficient, and I always send pictures electronically when I have a choice. The procedure for attaching an image file to an email message is essentially the same regardless of what email program you use; in this task, we'll use Microsoft Outlook.

Click to attach the image file to the email message.

You can email image files using any mail client.

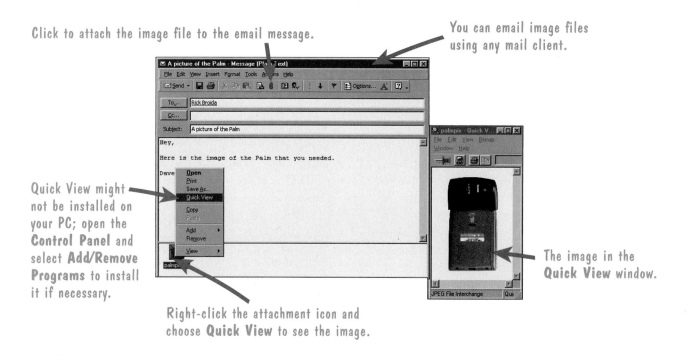

Quick View might not be installed on your PC; open the **Control Panel** and select **Add/Remove Programs** to install it if necessary.

The image in the **Quick View** window.

Right-click the attachment icon and choose **Quick View** to see the image.

Email Weirdness

You might find that some email attachments (such as image files) come out as gibberish on some people's computers. When that happens, there's usually a mismatch between the two systems' email-encoding formats. The two most common encoding techniques are called **UUENCODE** and **MIME**. Find the configuration for your mail program's encoding options and try changing from one to the other if your recipient can't read your image attachments.

1 Create a New Message

With Microsoft Outlook set to the **Inbox** view, click the **New** button in the Outlook toolbar to open a new, blank email message.

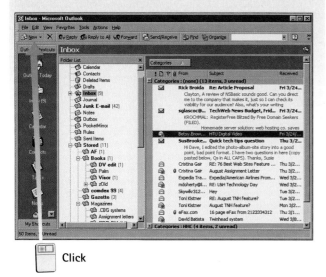

Click

2 Fill in the Message

Fill in the header information, such as the recipient's email address and the subject line. Then type the message body.

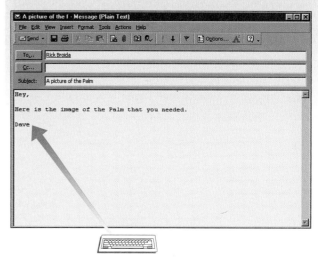

3 Attach the Image

Choose **Insert, File** from the message's menu and select the image file you want to attach from your hard drive. Click **Insert**. Alternatively, you can drag the image directly from the desktop to the message window. An icon appears at the bottom of the message window, showing that a file has been attached to the email message.

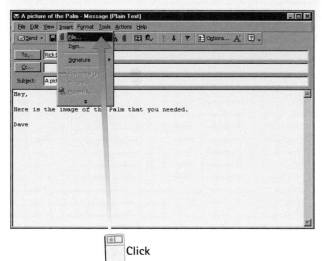

Click

4 Send the Message

When you're ready to send the email message and its attachment, click the **Send** button in the message toolbar.

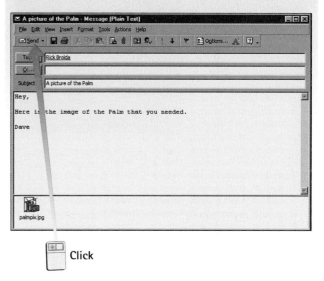

Click

End

How to Add Still Images to Video

You can mix still images with video in your movies very easily. Still images can be used to fill in gaps between video clips caused by long audio clips (as we saw in Part 6 of the book). You can also use several still images to create a digital slideshow. The possibilities, in fact, are endless.

A still image.

Make sure that images are 720×480 or they'll be distorted when they become part of a video clip.

Click here to grab a still from a video.

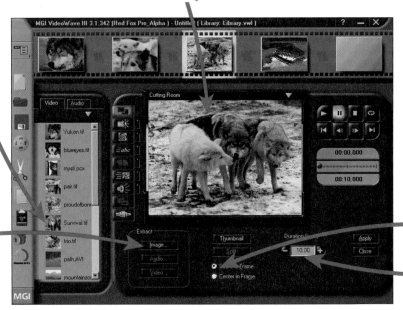

If the image is distorted, click here to center it in the frame.

Edit the duration of the image.

Check Your File Size

Remember to match image file sizes to the video you are making. If you are creating a digital video, for instance, import your images at 720×480 pixels. You might need to edit your image files in a program such as Paint Shop Pro to adjust the file size before you can import the image file into VideoWave.

1 Drag the Image V

In VideoWave, images can be handled the same as video clips. Drag an image from the Library to the Viewscreen.

Drag   Drop

2 Change the Duration V

By default, images in VideoWave appear for five seconds. To change that, click the **Cutting Room** button and set the **Duration** to any value. When you're done, click the **Apply** button.

1 Put it in the Timeline P

In Premiere, you can add an image to your project by dragging it from the **Project** window to the **Timeline**.

Drop

Drag

2 Change the Duration P

To lengthen or shorten the length of time the image displays, position the pointer at the right edge of the image track and drag it to any length of time you desire. Alternatively, right-click the image in the **Timeline** and choose **Duration** from the shortcut menu. Specify the desired length.

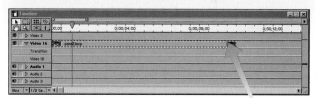

 Drag

End

Creating a Video Slide Show

A few years ago, it became popular to take a collection of 35mm slides and prints to the local photo shop and have the "experts" there convert the box of images into a slide show on VHS, complete with a soundtrack. Now you can do that yourself. You can convert those dusty old slides into a format that's easier to watch, so that everyone can appreciate the photographic archive of your life. Here's how.

Add transitions.

Stills.

Title slide.

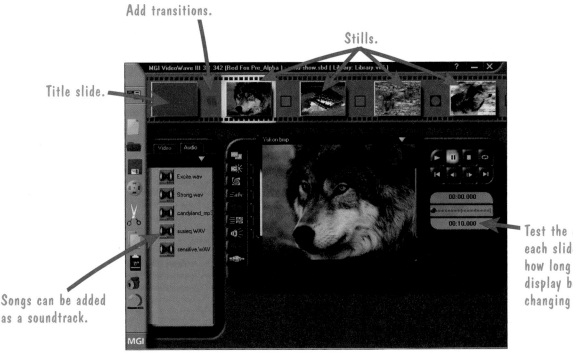

Test the duration of each slide to see how long it should display before changing slides.

Songs can be added as a soundtrack.

Slide Show Tips

Slide shows are a great way to preserve pictures in a format everyone can appreciate. Here are some tips to keep in mind when creating your video slide show:

- A good length of time to display each slide is about 10 seconds.
- Use a consistent transition after each slide. If you use a dozen different effects, the show can look like a student art project.
- If you use music from CDs, remember that the video must be intended for your personal use only.
- Try to match the music to the theme of the slides. Organize the slides by the music you'll be playing.
- Keep the total length of the slide show under about 20 minutes. If you have more slides, consider making more than one show.

1 Prepare Your Images

You're going to create a slide show on videotape for your friends and family—so start with the pictures. Scan your prints or slides into your PC and organize them in a single folder so that they're easy to get to.

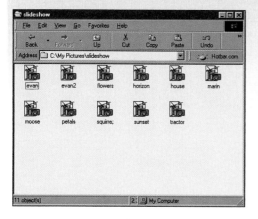

2 Start Fresh

Clear the VideoWave Storyline of any old clips that might be stored there by choosing **Storyline, New** from the menu button. If necessary, also delete clips you don't need from the Library.

Click

3 Import the Pictures

Click the list menu arrow in the Library and choose **Add Files**. Select all the images you created in Step 1 and load them into the Library.

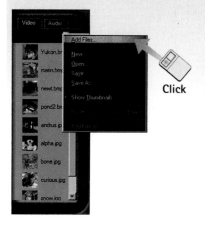

Click

4 Set the Time Preferences

By default, still images display in VideoWave for five seconds—but that's probably too short for a slide show. Click the menu button and choose **Preferences**. In the **Preferences** dialog box, set the **Default Still Image Duration** to whatever time you prefer (something along the lines of 10 seconds should be good).

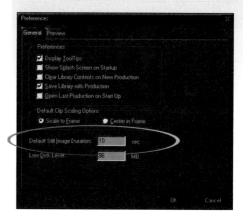

continues

Creating a Video Slide Show Continued

5 Add the Images

Drag the images from the Library to the Storyline. Arrange the images in the order you want your slide show to unfold.

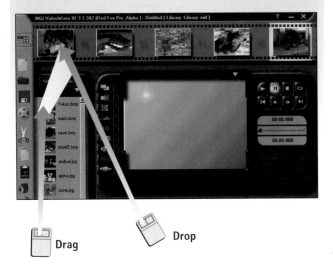

Drag   Drop

6 Add Transitions

Your slide show will probably benefit from some transitions. Double-click the transition placeholder between panels and add a simple transition—such as a fade—between each set of slides.

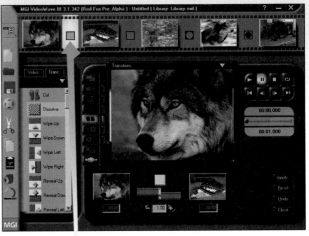

Double-click

7 Add Titles and Credits

Using the procedures presented in Part 5 of this book, create a color panel with introductory titles at the start of the show; add rolling credits to the end of the production.

8 Select the Show

Now that all the visuals are in place, you need to know how much music to prepare for the production. To learn that, hold down the **Shift** key and click to select all the panels in the Storyline. The entire Storyline should appear highlighted.

Shift + Click

9 Find the Length

With the slide show selected, click the **Last Frame** button in the VCR controls. You should see the total length of the show displayed. This value represents approximately how much music you have to prepare for the show.

Click

10 Save Your Work

By now, you've invested a lot of time in the slide show; it's at least halfway done. Save your work by choosing **Storyline, Save As** from the menu button. Give the slide show a name and click **OK** to keep your work safe on disk.

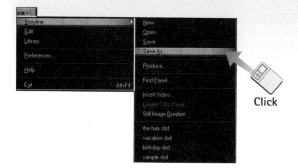

Click

11 Record the Music

Click the **Capture** button and follow the steps in Task 1 of Part 6, "How to Capture a Song from CD," to record selected tracks from CDs to the Library. If you acquire music this way, remember that copyright laws permit you to play this music only for personal use.

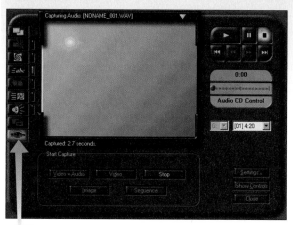

 Click

12 Display the Title

Drag the title panel to the Viewscreen. We're going to add a song to this panel to start the soundtrack for the slide show.

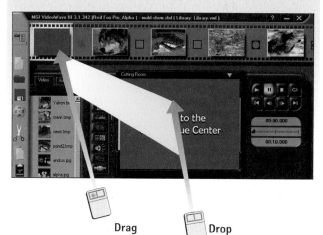

Drag   **Drop**

continues

13 Go to the Audio Studio

Click the **Audio Studio** button to begin your work with the audio portion of the slide show.

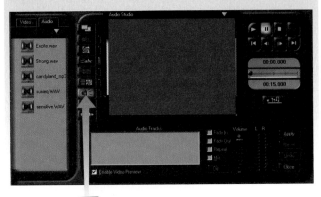

 Click

14 Apply the First Song

Drag the first song from the **Audio** tab of the Library to the **Audio Tracks** list in the Audio Studio console. Because you want this song to start playing right away, just click **Apply**.

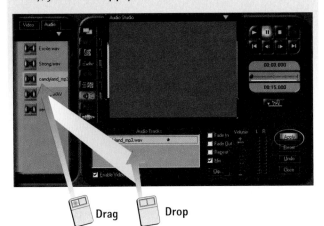

 Drag   Drop

15 Find the Next Slide

Depending on the length of the first song, it may span many slides. Check the length of the song to see which slide it ends in. You can determine the length of an audio clip by right-clicking it and choosing **Properties**.

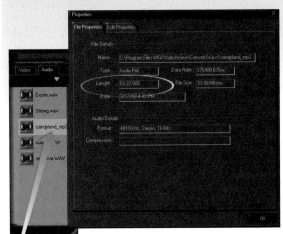

Right-click

16 Display the Next Slide

After you determine when the first song ends, go to the appropriate slide and drag it from the Storyline into the Viewscreen.

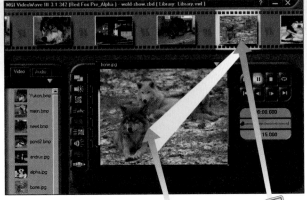

Drop   Drag

17 Go to the Audio Studio

With the slide in which the music will transition from one song to another displayed in the Viewscreen, click the **Audio Studio** button to return to your work with the audio portion of the slide show.

Click

18 Add the Next Song

Drag the next song you want to hear during the slide show into the **Audio Tracks** list. You should see two tracks listed: the first song, which ends sometime in this slide, and the song you just added.

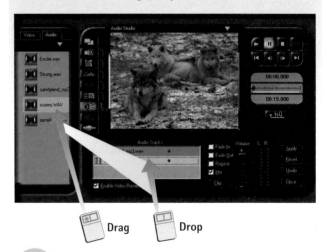

Drag   Drop

19 Start the New Song

As it stands now, both songs will play simultaneously when this slide appears. To get the second song to play when the first one ends, click the first song and drag the brown dot of the slider to a point just after the song ends (as indicated by the white line). Then click the second song and click the **Set Effect Start Position** button. The second song won't start until this point. Click **Apply**.

20 Repeat the Process

Repeat Steps 15 through 19 to add songs and delay their start points as many times as necessary until your slide show is complete. For the last slide, you might have to clip the song short and add a fade-out effect (refer to Part 6, "Working with Audio," for information). Your slide show is complete!

End

Task

PART 8

Producing Videotape

*A*fter hours of filming, capturing, and editing audio and video, you finally have a finished project on your PC. It doesn't do anyone much good there, though. In fact, so far in the book, I haven't really told you how to produce a watchable movie. Instead, I've had you arrange clips, add titles, use special effects...but the video isn't finished and you can't sit someone down—even in front of the computer—to watch your creation. That's because VideoWave (or Premiere) needs to *render* your raw files into a finished film.

After the movie has been rendered (another term you may see used for this process is *produced*), you can watch the video as a full-screen film on your PC. That's great, but most likely, you'll want to copy the video onto tape and distribute it to friends, family, or co-workers. In the following tasks, I talk about how to make videotape from a finished production. If you prefer to burn the movie onto CD-ROM or copy it to the Web, hold on to your hat! We'll do that in Part 9 of this book. ●

How to Prepare Your Video for Tape

Before you can copy your production to tape, you must *produce* the movie. Producing the movie renders it in its final form and stores it on your hard disk. The produced video becomes the high-quality master from which you can make any number of copies—and those copies will be every bit as good as

the first copy. In this task, I explain the process for producing your movie in VideoWave. In Premiere, the process varies depending on the kind of video capture hardware you have in your PC. Check the documentation that came with your FireWire card for details.

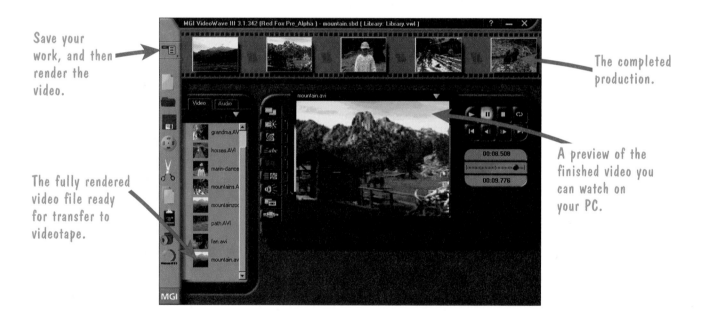

Save your work, and then render the video.

The completed production.

A preview of the finished video you can watch on your PC.

The fully rendered video file ready for transfer to videotape.

Prepping Premiere

As I mentioned in Part 3, Task 5, "How to Capture Video," Adobe Premiere uses project settings for your desired output right from the start. Make sure that your project is configured for DV output when you begin the project using the dialog boxes that appear when you start the program.

Producing Part of a Production

Thanks to the magic of digital video editing, you don't have to produce the entire movie. For example, you might want to produce just the first few scenes to make sure that your settings are right. After all, it can take hours to produce the entire movie, and you don't want to find out after an evening of rendering that you chose the wrong format and that your video has been rendered to a small Web-style window instead of in full screen for videotape.

1 Save Your Work

The first step—before you render the video—is to save the production. From the menu button, choose **Storyline, Save**. If anything happens during the production, you now have a good backup to work from.

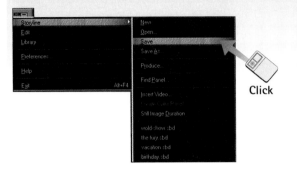

Click

2 Select the Panels

You might want to produce only part of the movie. If that's the case, Shift-click to select the panels in the Storyline that you want to appear in the movie. Otherwise, move on to the next step.

Shift + Click

3 Start the Production

Click the menu button and choose **Storyline, Produce**. The **Produce Movie** wizard appears.

Click

4 Choose the Panels

If you want to produce just the panels you selected in Step 2, select the **Highlighted Clips Only** option. Otherwise, select the **Entire Storyline** option.

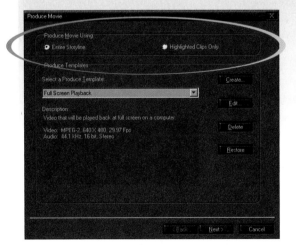

continues

5 Pick a Template

Now you have to select the correct settings to produce the movie. If you're making a movie in DV format (using a DV camcorder and a FireWire cable), choose **DV** from the **Select a Produce Template** list. If you are using an analog camcorder, choose **Full Screen Playback**.

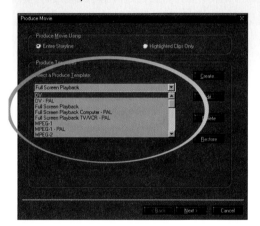

6 Enter Edit Mode

Most of the time, you don't need to tweak the Edit settings. But if you have special needs (for example, if you want to change the size of the rendered movie), click the **Edit** button to open the **Settings** dialog box. We use the Edit feature in the next part of the book.

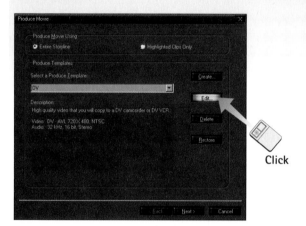

Click

7 Make Changes

In the **Settings** dialog box, you will find options such as stereo and mono audio or PAL and NTSC playback that you can choose from. Make any changes you want and click the **Finish** button to return to the **Produce Movie** dialog box.

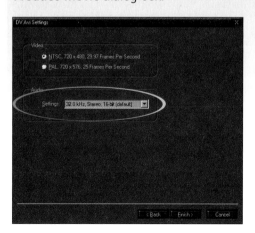

8 Go to the Summary

Now that you've selected a template, click the **Next** button to go to the **Summary Page**, where you can name the file and prepare to render the movie.

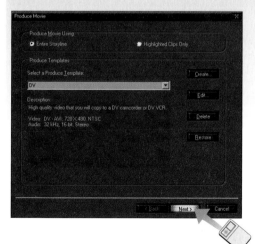

Click

9 Name the File

In the **Summary Page**, give the video file a name. If necessary, use the **Browse** button to locate where you want to save the video. This step takes all the pieces of the video you have made earlier in the book—the clips, transitions, titles, and music—and renders them into a single video file that conforms to the template settings you just made. In this case, we're using a template to make a videotape, but we could just as easily render the production files into a format for the Web or a CD-ROM.

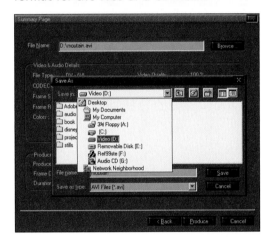

10 Produce It!

It's the moment of truth: Click the **Produce** button. The video will be rendered to your hard drive. Don't be surprised if it takes a while—maybe even hours. You can track the video's progress onscreen.

11 Watch the Preview

When the production process is complete, the video appears in the Library and in the Viewscreen. Click the **Play** button to watch the completed movie in the Viewscreen.

 Click

12 See It Full Size

Alternatively, you can use Windows Explorer to find the movie file on your hard drive (the file has the extension **AVI**) and double-click it. The movie should open in a Media Player window and play at its full size.

End

How to Copy the Finished Video to Tape

Now that the video has been created, edited, and produced, all that remains is to copy it to videotape. After making a copy on DV tape, you can use that copy to make an infinite number of copies on VHS tape, as you'll see in the next task.

Here's the finished video playing on a DV camcorder.

Record to a digital videotape if possible for the highest quality video.

Use the video-out port on your camcorder to make copies on your TV's analog VCR.

NTSC Versus PAL

If you've never worked with video before, terms such as NTSC and PAL might seem really confusing. Why would you use one format instead of the other? The answer is actually pretty easy. The two formats are similar, but the resolution and display frequency are slightly different. NTSC is the standard for transmitting and displaying video in the United States. If you're in Europe, you use PAL or SECAM. In general, you can't take a video in one of these formats and play it in a VCR made for a different format.

1 Load the Video

If the finished video isn't already loaded in the Viewscreen, drag it from the Library to the Viewscreen now. If you just finished producing the video, it should be in the Viewscreen already.

Drag   Drop

2 Connect the Camera

Attach your camcorder to the FireWire or video connector on your PC. Refer to the documentation for your particular camcorder for specific details.

3 Turn On the Camera

Turn on your camera and set it to **Play**, not to **Record**. The software on your PC controls the camera and can write to tape only if the camera is turned to the **Play** setting.

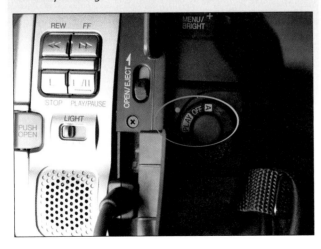

4 Insert a Tape

Make sure that you have a fresh, blank tape installed in your camera. If you accidentally overwrite existing video footage, there's no undo button—you can't get it back.

continues

5 Use AC Power

Connect your camcorder to its AC adapter and plug it into a wall outlet. You don't want to rely on battery power when making the video master because a low battery can ruin your tape.

6 Choose Output to Video

In VideoWave, click the **Output to Video** button to switch to the Output mode.

 Click

7 Set the Correct Output

From the **Output** list, choose **DV Output** if you're writing the video to a DV camcorder. If you're recording to analog video, choose **Full Screen**.

8 Find the Right Spot on the Tape

Use the VCR controls in VideoWave or on the camcorder itself to set the tape to the point at which you want to start recording. Most of the time, you'll probably just want to rewind to the beginning of the physical tape.

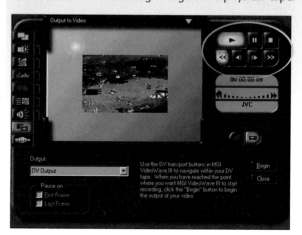

9 Start Recording: Digital Video

If you are using a DV camcorder, click the **Begin** button when you're ready to start recording the PC file to the DV tape in the camcorder. VideoWave automatically starts the camcorder, and the video will record on the tape.

 Click

10 Start Recording: Analog Video

If you're using an analog camcorder, you must start recording on the camera manually and then click the **Begin** button in VideoWave. You can also click the checkbox for **Pause on First Frame**. If you do that, the very first frame of the video holds until you press the spacebar. You might want to hold the first frame because it can take several seconds for the tape on your camcorder to spool up, get past the leader, and begin recording. If your first frame is a black panel or the title, you can write that to the tape for several seconds so that you don't accidentally lose any of the video that follows.

Click

11 Check Your Video

When the recording is complete, press the **Stop** button on the camcorder, rewind the tape, and press **Play** on the camcorder. You should see the finished product in the camera's viewfinder.

12 Close the Output to Video Screen

When you're done, click the **Close** button to close the **Output to Video** screen and return to the standard Viewscreen. Congratulations, you've made a video! At this point, you can safely delete the video files from your PC's hard disk and make subsequent copies from the digital tape. If you don't have a digital camcorder and are instead making copies directly to VHS tape, you might want to keep the files on your PC to make additional copies. Remember that, unlike copies from digital tape, copies from VHS are "lossy" and lose resolution and image quality with each copy you make.

End

How to Work with a Videotape Master

The first physical videotape you record from your PC video file is known as a *master*. The master tape is a high-quality source to which you should return whenever you want to make more copies. Of course, you could use the file on your hard drive as a master, but you won't want to keep that file forever because it takes up so much storage space. Just two or three videos, and your whole hard drive would be filled with old master videos! Instead, connect your camcorder to the VCR and dub copies.

The DV tape is digital and makes the highest quality master.

The DV master t ape is identical to the video file on your PC.

Copies made from VHS tapes degrade from copy to copy.

Quality and Generations

Every time you make a copy of a copy of a VHS tape, the quality degrades substantially. Consider this: A standard VHS videotape has only half the resolution of a regular television broadcast, and you lose another 15% of the image quality every time you make a copy. That's why it's important to start with a high-quality master tape (such as a DV tape) and only make copies from that. If you are working with analog video, the master is actually the production file on the computer; the final videotape you make is already second generation. If you dub a copy from that, you're now looking at a third-generation tape, which most people consider to be at the very fringe of acceptability.

1 Wire the VCR

To record from your camcorder to your VCR, you'll need to get analog video and audio cables. Most likely, a set came with your camera or VCR. If not, buy a set from a local stereo store. Connect the **Video-Out** and **Audio-Out** jacks on the camcorder to the **Audio-In** and **Video-In** jacks on the VCR.

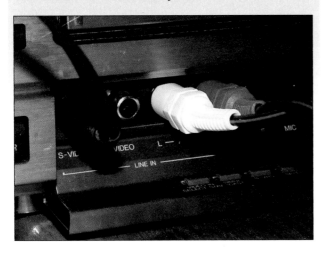

2 Insert Tapes

Put the master tape in your camcorder and a blank videotape in your VCR. Rewind both tapes to the appropriate points to start recording.

3 Set the VCR

Now you must configure your VCR to "see" the camcorder. You need to set the VCR's channel to an **External Input**, usually indicated by the characters **Ext** or **AU**. Refer to your VCR's documentation and experiment until you can see output from the camcorder on the TV.

4 Start Recording

Start recording on the VCR and wait a few seconds until you're past the non-recordable leader at the beginning of the tape. Then press **Play** on the camcorder. The video should be copied from the camcorder to the videotape in the VCR.

End

Task

Publishing Video to the Web and CD-ROM

In the digital age, video is a very versatile product. Sure, you can copy it to videotape (as we did in the previous part of the book), but you can also include it on Web pages, distribute it to friends or co-workers on CD-ROM, or even include it in a PowerPoint presentation. Web pages are a great convenient mechanism for letting people see your video because all you need to do is tell them where to surf. The downside? Imagine quality is lower, and playback might be jerky if your visitor has a slow modem. In the tasks in this part of the book, I'll show you how to incorporate video in Web pages and CD-ROMs.

How to Prepare Your Video for the Web

TASK 1

Before you can put your video production on the Web, you need to first produce the movie—just as you did for videotape in the previous part of the book. Producing the video renders your movie in its final form and stores it on your hard disk. After rendering the movie, you can then move it to the Internet. In this task, I explain the process for producing your movie in VideoWave. In Premiere, the process varies depending on the kind of video capture hardware in your PC. Check the documentation that came with your FireWire card for details.

Video is being rendered.

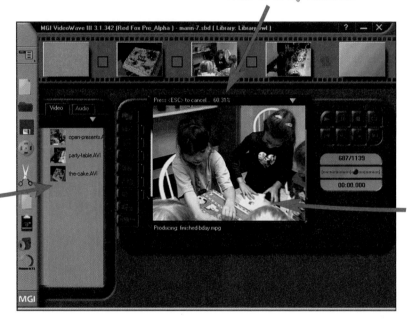

The finished video will be copied to the Library.

Video must be rendered in a compressed format for the Web.

Bandwidth Concerns

Planning to publish your movie on the Internet? Keep in mind that although you might have a fast cable modem or DSL connection (I don't know that you really do...I'm just guessing) to view Web pages at high speed, many other folks are still plugging along with 28.8Kbps and 56Kbps modems. Make sure that you keep your movie short—well under a megabyte—so that it doesn't take all day to download. Also consider making the movie *stream* (see Task 4).

Choose the Right Format

When you render a video for the Web or CD, choose a format (such as MPEG-1) that most people have installed on their computers. Keep in mind that few people have MPEG-2, so you should avoid that format.

1 Save Your Work

Before you render the video, you should save the production. From the menu button, choose **Storyline, Save**. Now, if anything happens during the production, you now have a good backup to work from.

Click

2 Select the Panels

You might want to produce only part of the movie. If that's the case, hold down the **Shift** key and click to select the panels in the Storyline that you want to appear in the movie. Otherwise, just move on to the next step.

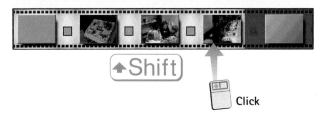

Click

3 Start the Production

From the menu button, choose **Storyline, Produce**. The **Produce Movie** wizard appears.

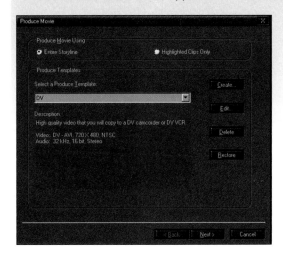

4 Choose the Panels

If you want to produce just the panels you selected in Step 2, choose the **Highlighted Clips Only** option. Otherwise, select the **Entire Storyline** option.

continues

5 Pick a Template

Now select the settings to produce the movie. The **Select a Produce Template** list provides a trio of pre-set Web video formats. Depending on how fast you think your audience's Internet connection is, pick from the **Web Video - Best Quality**, **Web Video - Good Quality**, and **Web Video - Minimum Size** options.

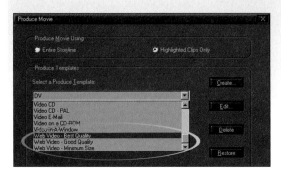

6 Enter Edit Mode

You can change the specific attributes of the Web Video template you selected by clicking the **Edit** button. You'll have to edit the settings to make sure that you'll be rendering the video into a size that's appropriate for the Web. Click **Edit**, and the **Settings** dialog box opens.

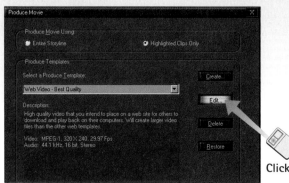

Click

7 Make Changes

In the **Settings** dialog box, click **Next**. On this page, the most important settings are **Bit Rate** and **Audio Channels**. Throttle the **Bit Rate** up or down to affect the quality of the video and the rate at which it plays. The **Audio Channel** option also affects the quality-to-download rate ratio. Make any changes you want and click the **Finish** button to return to the **Produce Movie** wizard.

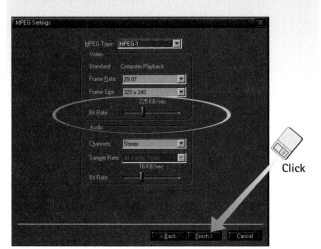

Click

8 Go to the Summary

Now that you have made any necessary changes to the video format, click the **Next** button. The **Summary Page** appears.

9 Name the File

On the **Summary Page** dialog box, name the file. If necessary, use the **Browse** button to find the location on the drive where you want to save the video file. Remember, the file you are about to produce combines the various production components you saved in Step 1 into a single, playable video file.

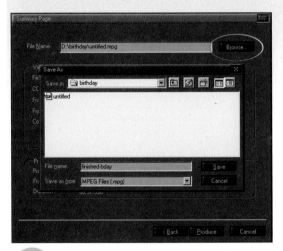

10 Produce It!

It's the moment of truth: Click the **Produce** button. The video will be rendered to your hard drive. Don't be surprised if this step takes a while—perhaps even hours. This is the number-crunching part of the process, in which all the bits are combined into a single file. You can track the video's progress onscreen.

11 Watch the Preview

When the production process is complete, the video will appear in the Library and in the Viewscreen. Click the **Play** button to watch the completed movie in the Viewscreen.

 Click

12 See It Full Size

Alternatively, you can use **My Computer** to find the file on your hard drive and double-click it (the file has the extension **MPG**). The movie should open in a Media Player window and play at its full size.

End

How to Insert a Movie into a Web Page

After you produce a movie that you want to display in a Web page, you're only halfway there. You still have to create the Web page itself and get the video file onto the Internet. In this task, you get your Web page ready and drop in the video you've prepared. Because Microsoft FrontPage is so popular, I've chosen to explain the process using that program; if you have another program, the procedure will be quite similar. By referring to this task and your Web editor's user manual, you should be able to figure out the process without too much trouble.

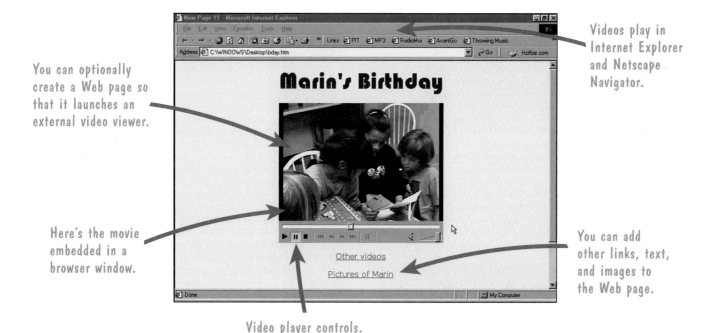

You can optionally create a Web page so that it launches an external video viewer.

Videos play in Internet Explorer and Netscape Navigator.

Here's the movie embedded in a browser window.

You can add other links, text, and images to the Web page.

Video player controls.

Optimizing Video for the Web

Posting a movie on the Internet probably means that it's been highly compressed to save space and bandwidth—when you produce your movie in VideoWave, for instance, you select a Web-friendly template so that the video is adequately compressed for playback on the Internet. To make your movie look its best on the Net, try some of these tips:

- **Minimize movement.** The less movement in the video, the more smoothly it plays back in compressed form.
- **Extend transitions.** Make those transitions longer. That way, they won't be destroyed by compression.
- **Make text really big.** If you use titles, make the text even bigger than usual so that the text is legible after the video is compressed.

1 Use FrontPage

The easiest way to get a video clip into a Web page is to use a Web design program such as Microsoft FrontPage. Most programs—including FrontPage—have built-in tools for generating a Web page with video clips.

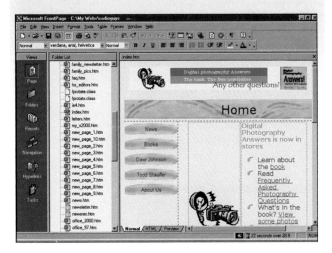

2 Insert the Plug-In

If you're using FrontPage, open the Web page you want to insert the clip into and choose **Insert, Advanced, Plug-In** from the menu. FrontPage uses the term *plug-in* to refer to any component (such as video) that needs a special viewer. The **Plug-In Properties** dialog box opens. Click the **Browse** button and select the video file you've already produced in VideoWave. Click **OK** to add this element to the page. Note that the video clip appears on the Web page as a plug icon.

Click

3 Size the Plug-In

Click to select the Plug-In icon on the Web page and drag its sizing handles to adjust the pane in which the video clip will play. Size the pane however you like, and be sure to use the **Preview** tab to see what the finished video will look like in the Web page.

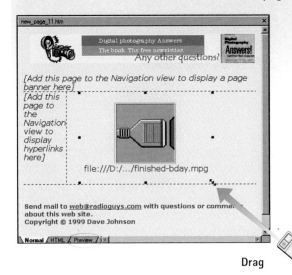

Drag

4 Do It Manually

If you are familiar with creating Web pages using HTML, you can include your video clip in a Web page by adding the following line of HTML code in your Web page:

```
<embed width="400" height="400" src="movie.mpg">
```

Remember to change the width and height values to match the size of your movie and set the **SRC** variable to the name of your video file.

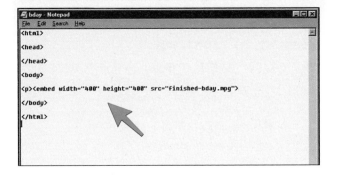

End

How to Upload the Movie to the Web

After you've created your Web page on your PC and included a video clip or two in the page, you might want to actually publish the Web page on the Internet. Only after this last, crucial step can you actually invite others to your Web site and let them view your video creation.

The program can automatically upload Web pages to the Internet.

FrontPage or another visual Web design program makes creating Web pages easy.

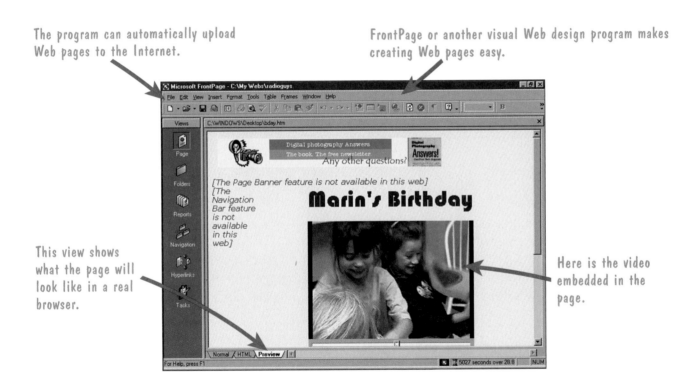

This view shows what the page will look like in a real browser.

Here is the video embedded in the page.

Beware of FrontPage

If you use FrontPage to upload your Web pages, don't make "manual" changes to your site with an FTP program, or you might confuse FrontPage and damage its knowledge about what's stored on your Web server. FrontPage likes to keep track of all the files on your Web site. This actually makes it easy for you to update your Web site because you can make changes to your site on your computer's hard drive and then tell FrontPage to make the appropriate changes to your Web site by "publishing changed files." If you change files manually using an FTP program, FrontPage can't tell what has changed and what hasn't. Consequently, it can do real damage to your published site if you later command it to publish changed files to the Web.

1 Do It the Automatic Way

If you are using a Web page authoring program such as FrontPage, the process of uploading the page to the Internet is pretty simple. The program tracks the location of all the files in your Web page—including your video files. Choose **File, Publish Web** from the menu to open the **Publish Web** dialog box.

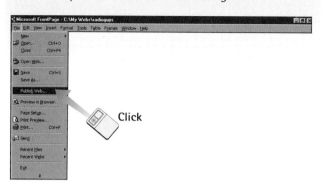

Click

2 Specify a Location

Enter the location to which you plan to publish the site—for example, you might enter your domain name. Then click the **Publish** button and let FrontPage do all the work.

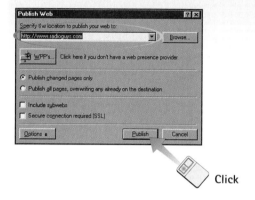

Click

3 Move It with FTP

If you're uploading the page to the Internet more manually than with a program like FrontPage, you need an FTP client. (I like a program called FTP Voyager.) Enter the **FTP site** name (the location where your Web site will be stored) along with your **User ID** and **Password**. Then connect to your site.

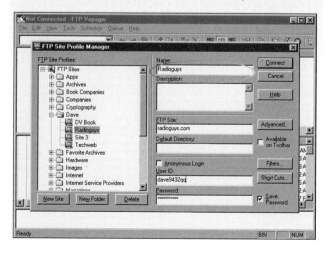

4 Copy the Video File

Use the FTP program to copy the video file to an appropriate folder at your Web site's domain. Be sure that the folder name and filename exactly match the names you used in your Web site's HTML code (as shown in Step 4 of the previous task).

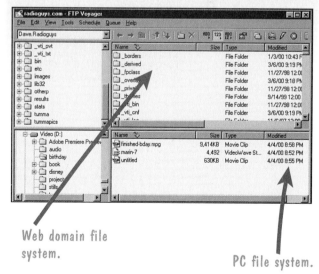

Web domain file system.

PC file system.

End

How to Upload the Movie to the Web   205

How to Prepare a Streaming Movie

The video you made and uploaded in Tasks 1, 2, and 3 must be downloaded from the Internet in its entirety before someone can watch it in a Web browser. If your audience has a slow Internet connection, the time spent downloading the video file is often more than the video clip is worth. As an alternative, you might want to use *streaming video* so that visitors to your Web site can watch the movie as it downloads. To stream video, you need to produce it in a special way in VideoWave, and then feed it into another (free) program called RealProducer, which I'll talk about in the next task.

Internet Explorer is the browser.

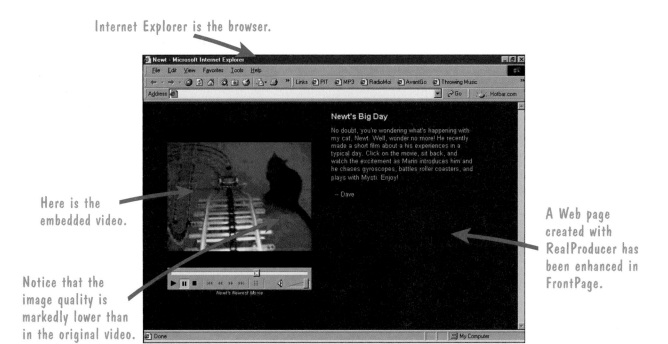

Here is the embedded video.

Notice that the image quality is markedly lower than in the original video.

A Web page created with RealProducer has been enhanced in FrontPage.

Finding Streaming Video

If you surf the Web very often, you no doubt know that streaming media is the preferred method for watching video and listening to music—it's more instantaneous than waiting for a file to download completely to your PC. If you want to look for streaming video on your own, the best starting place is **www.real.com**. This site has the necessary viewer software as well as untold riches of movie files to watch.

Free Web Storage

Looking for somewhere to store your streaming movie? PopCast.com is a Web site that lets you put your movies on the Web for free.

1 Create a New Template

With your movie loaded in the VideoWave Storyline, choose **Storyline, Produce** from the menu button to open the **Produce Movie** wizard. By default, VideoWave creates movies only in MPEG format, but RealProducer requires an AVI movie. The first time you create a streaming movie, click the **Create** button to make a new template.

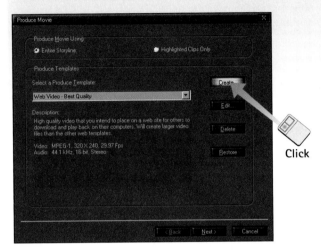

Click

2 Name the Template

In the **Template Name** field of the **Create Produce Template** dialog box, give the template you are about to create a name—something like **Streaming Video**—so that you can find this template again in the future. From the **File Type** list, choose **AVI Compressed**. Click **Next**.

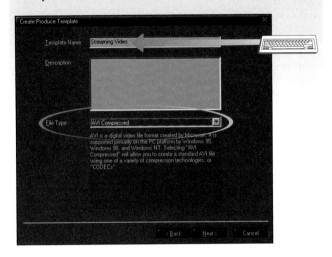

3 Set Video Options

This next dialog box, **AVI Settings**, looks intimidating, but you can accept the defaults. Make sure that you are using **Indeo** video compression, that the frame size is **320×240**, and that the **Quality** slider is set to **High (100%)**. Click the **Finish** button to return to the **Produce Movie** wizard.

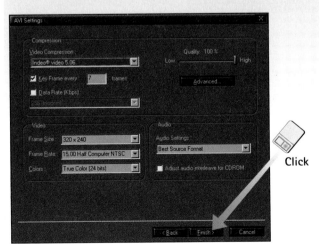

Click

4 Produce Your Movie

Click the **Next** button to go to the **Summary Page**. Type a name for your movie and click the **Produce** button to create your movie file. Note that the movie isn't in streaming format yet; you have to import it into the next task and finish the job.

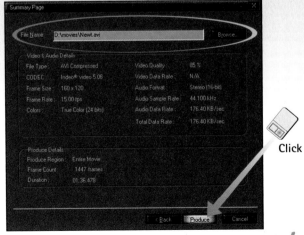

Click

End

How to Create a Streaming Movie

Streaming video is a popular way to deliver audio and video on the Internet because you don't have to download huge data files to experience the multimedia effects. To create streaming media of your own, you'll need RealProducer, a free program found at **www.real.com**. The basic version of this program enables you to take a completed video, convert it to streaming format, and post it to a Web site. To actually watch the streaming video after it has been published to the Web, your audience needs a copy of RealPlayer (also a free download). Thankfully, RealPlayer comes preinstalled on most PCs, so they're ready to rock right from the start.

You can download RealPlayer for free from www.real.com.

Player controls.

Here you can watch the streaming video.

Click here to change the size of the video.

Sprucing Up Your Movie Page

RealProducer has a Web page publisher built in, which makes creating a complete Web page with the streaming video file already embedded easy to upload to the Web. But you don't have to settle for RealProducer's plain vanilla page. You can take the Web page that RealProducer creates for you and import it into FrontPage or another Web design program to add links, background graphics, additional text, and any other features you expect to find on a page at your Web site. You can then upload the completed page to the Web using your Web editor (such as FrontPage) or an FTP program.

1 Start RealProducer

After you have created a complete movie in AVI format in VideoWave, start your copy of RealProducer. In the **New Session** dialog box that appears when you launch the program, choose **Record From File** and click **OK**.

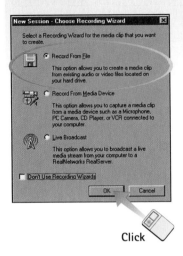

Click

2 Find the Video

On the first page of the **Recording Wizard**, click the **Browse** button and choose the filename of the streaming video file you created in the last task. Click Next.

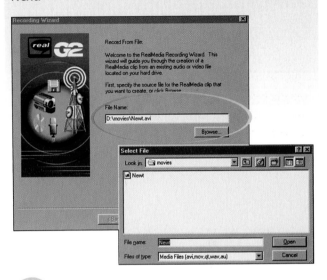

3 Name the File

Now enter the details about your video that will appear on the Web page. Give the file a title, name the author, type a brief description of the video file, and enter some appropriate *keywords*. The keywords make it easier for Web surfers to find your video in search engines. Click **Next**.

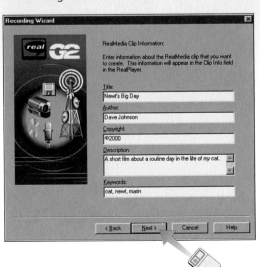

Click

4 Choose a Server Type

Because you're probably posting this video to your own Web server and are not expecting thousands of people to flock to it, choose the **Single-rate for Web Servers** option and click **Next**. (If you had a high demand for your movies, you would want to use a special server that could deliver the movie to many people simultaneously.)

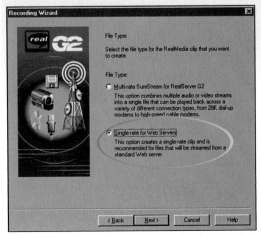

continues

How to Create a Streaming Video Continued

5 Choose a Target Audience

RealProducer assumes that you know something about the kind of people who will view your movie. Select the kind of Internet connection you expect most of your viewers to have. If you don't know the modem speeds of your audience, a safe bet is **56K Modem**. Click **Next**.

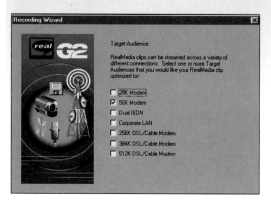

6 Choose Audio Quality

Select the option that best represents the kind of audio in your movie. The **Stereo Music** option takes up more of the available bandwidth than **Voice Only**, leaving less bandwidth available for the video stream. For most videos, **Voice with Background Music** is your best bet because it balances the sound quality with video quality pretty well. Click **Next**.

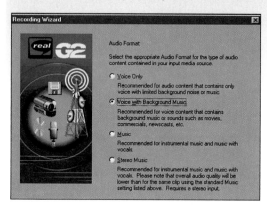

7 Choose Video Quality

Select the option that best represents the kind of video in your movie. **Normal Motion Video** is usually a good compromise. Don't choose **Slide Show** if you want the video to appear as a motion picture. Click **Next**.

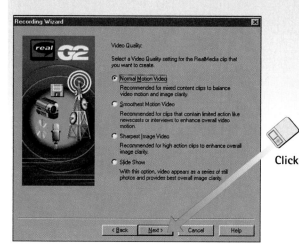

 Click

8 Name Your Video

Choose a filename and location for your movie. This file, bearing the **.rm** file extension, is the hyper-compressed streaming video file that was rendered based on the VideoWave produced file. It is the file that will be uploaded to your Web site. Click **Next**.

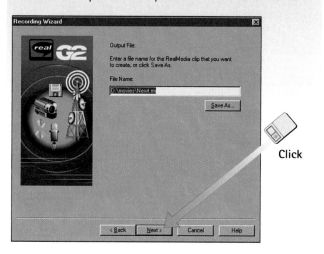

 Click

9 Verify Your Settings

The next dialog box displays all the data about your movie. Check it over to make sure that it is all correct; you can use the **Back** button to make changes to these options. When you're satisfied with your movie settings, click the **Finish** button.

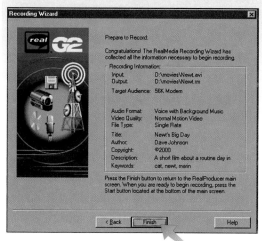

Click

10 Ready to Produce

After the **Recording Wizard** goes away, you finally see the main **RealProducer** window. This view gives you one last chance to make any changes to your video before you produce it.

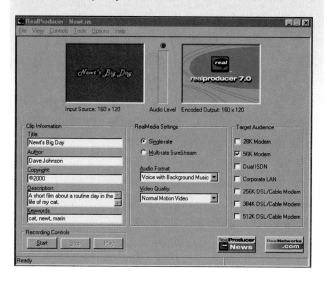

11 Start the Encoding

Click the **Start** button. The video will play and encode itself into a streaming video file.

Click

12 Post It to the Web

After the file is complete, you can upload it to your Web site. RealProducer includes a wizard for creating and publishing the streaming video file in the **Tools** menu.

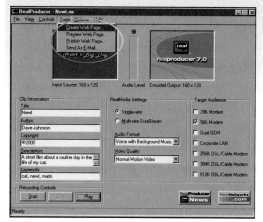

End

How to Put Your Video on CD-ROM

Creating a video for CD-ROM is very similar to working with video files for the Web. Both are sensitive to data rate—if you try to play a very large, high-resolution video from the Web or from CD-ROM, you will experience choppiness, stutters, and frustrating results. Most people have fairly fast CD-ROM drives these days, however, so it's not too hard to play back good-looking video directly from CD-ROM. Here's how to create that video.

Record on CD-R discs; CD-RW discs might not play in everyone's CD-ROM drive.

The 650MB of space on a standard CD can store a lot of video.

Special, inexpensive label makers can make your CD look professionally published, unlike the handwritten note on this CD.

Using a Front End on the CD-ROM

If you plan to distribute your movie on CD-ROMs, you don't have to just copy the video file to the disc and let users search for the movie file using Windows Explorer. Instead, build your movie files into Web pages using the Web page feature in RealProducer and copy the complete "Web site" you've made to CD-ROM. When the users of your CD start your on-disc Web page, they can click their way around as if they were navigating a real Web site. It's an elegant way to complete a CD-ROM.

The Right Hardware

If you plan to "burn" CD-ROMs and distribute the discs to friends and family, you'll need a CD-RW drive. Different from a standard CD-ROM drive, CD-RW drives can actually create CDs from blank discs. Although CD-RW drives can write to both CD-R (recordable once) and CR-RW (rewritable, erasable) discs, only CD-R discs are readable in everyone else's drives. The lesson here is to make copies of your videos on CD-R.

1 Start the Production

From the VideoWave menu button, choose **Storyline, Produce**. The **Produce Movie** wizard appears.

2 Pick a Template

Experiment with templates to find what works for you, but a good place to start is with the **Video on a CD-ROM** option. If you don't like the default settings, click the **Edit** button and make the video bigger (that is, change its physical size on the screen during playback) or increase the bit rate, which determines the overall image quality.

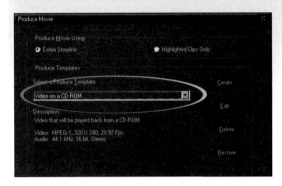

3 Produce the Video

Click the **Next** button to move to the **Summary Page**. Click the **Produce** button, and the video will be rendered to your hard disk. Don't be surprised if this step takes a while—perhaps even hours. You can track the video's progress onscreen.

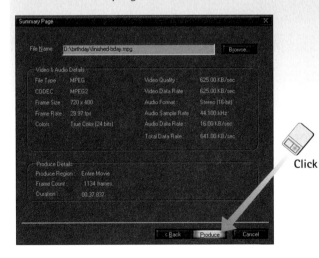

Click

4 Burn a CD-ROM

When the video is complete, use the software that came with your CD-RW drive to copy it to a blank CD-R disc. A program such as Adaptec's Easy CD Creator is an excellent choice for copying files to CD-R discs.

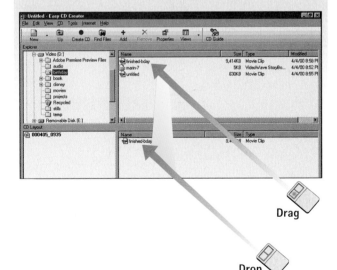

Drag

Drop

End

Project 3

Creating a Video for the Web

If you've created videos using previous tasks in this book, you should already know how to create your video, add the effects, and produce it. But getting the video onto a Web site is a different matter altogether. Actually, it's pretty easy to do. In this project, I show you how to take your finished video and convert it into a streaming movie that plays directly from the Web. Best of all, you can do it with free tools that are easy to use. You'll need VideoWave and a completed video production (a movie), the RealProducer software, and a Web site onto which you can upload the files. Follow along, and you'll learn what to do with these raw ingredients.

Here's an example of streaming video.

Internet Explorer and Netscape Navigator both play streaming video.

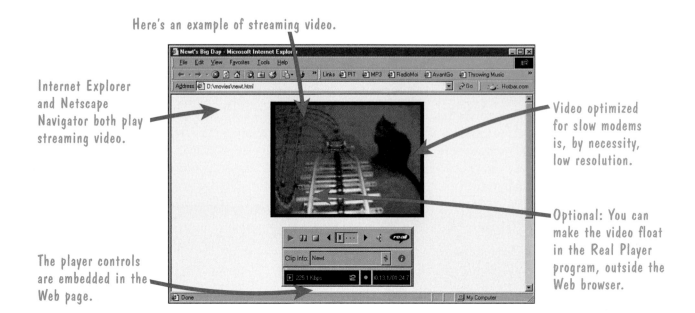

Video optimized for slow modems is, by necessity, low resolution.

Optional: You can make the video float in the Real Player program, outside the Web browser.

The player controls are embedded in the Web page.

Stream or Download?

In this project, we build a video and then stream it on the Web. That's because I prefer streaming movies on the Internet. But there are occasions in which you would want to upload an MPEG file instead of a streaming video AVI file to the Web so that visitors have to download it before viewing it. Here are some examples of when to use each type of file format:

- Use MPEG if you want higher image quality than you can get with a streaming Real file.

- Use MPEG if you want your visitors to be able to save a copy of the movie on their own hard drives.

- Use AVI if you want the highest possible quality video image—it'll look better than a comparable MPEG movie. Remember, though, that an AVI movie will probably be huge.

- Use Streaming Real format if you want your visitors to be able to see the movie in real-time instead of first downloading the entire movie to their hard disk.

1 Complete the Video

In VideoWave, create your movie, complete with titles, transitions, and any other elements you want. Save the file and then choose **Storyline, Produce** from the menu button. The **Produce Movie** dialog box opens.

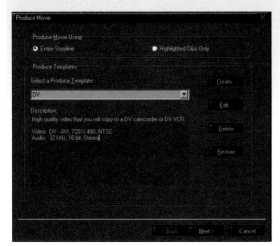

2 Use the AVI Template

Publish your movie using the AVI template you created in Part 9, Task 4, "How to Prepare a Streaming Movie." Remember that the file must be in AVI format if it is to work as a streaming video file.

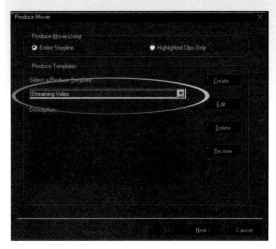

3 Load the File in RealProducer

After your movie has been rendered in VideoWave, it's time to load it into RealProducer. Start the program; when the **New Session** dialog box appears, choose **Record from File** and then select the AVI file you just created.

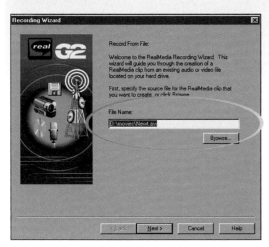

4 Add the Details

In the **Recording Wizard**, enter the title, author, keywords, and other details about your video. Then click **Next** and select the **Single-rate for Web Servers** option. Click **Next** again.

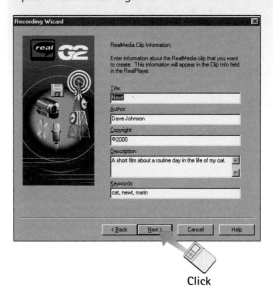

Click

continues

5 Choose the Video Quality

The next three dialog boxes help determine the over-all video quality as it streams from the Web to your viewers' screens. Choose the average connection speed you expect people to use (**56K** is a good default), and then click **Next** to choose the amount of bandwidth RealProducer should dedicate to both audio and video. Click **Next.**

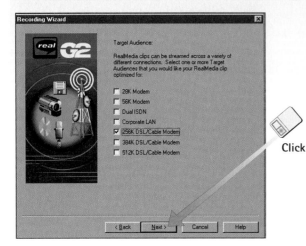

Click

6 Name the File

Give the streaming video file you are creating a name and select the location on your hard drive where you want to store the file. Click **Next** to see a summary of your settings, and then click **Finish.**

Click

7 Produce the Video

With all the settings done, click the **Start** button to render the streaming video file.

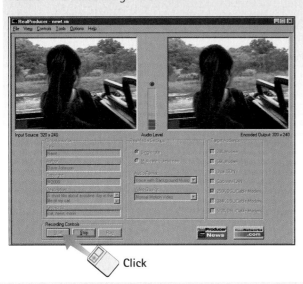

Click

8 Create a Web Page

Choose **Tools, Create Web Page** from the RealProducer menu. This option starts the **Web Page Wizard,** which you can use to make a video-enabled Web page.

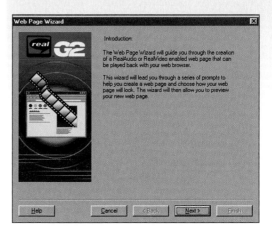

9 Locate the Video File

Click **Next** to see the **Media File** page of the wizard. Click **Browse** to select the streaming video file you just created and then click **Next** again.

10 Select a Player

Choose which kind of media player you want to use. You can have the video embedded in the page itself, or the RealPlayer application can be launched and run on top of the Web page. When you have made your selection, click **Next**. I suggest that you let the RealPlayer application launch outside the browser because that arrangement enables you to create more attractive Web pages.

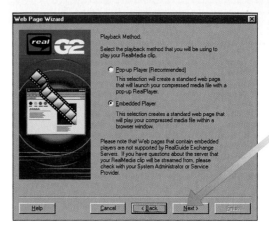

Click

11 Add a Caption

Type the caption you want to appear on the Web page to identify the video content. This caption appears below the video window on the Web page. Click **Next**.

12 Name the Web Page

Choose a filename and a location on your hard drive for the Web page you are creating. Click **Next**.

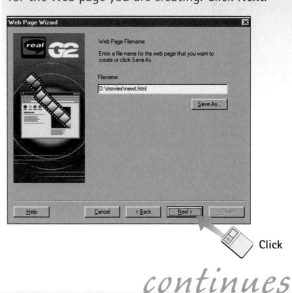
Click

continues

13 Preview and Finish

If you want to preview the Web page in your default browser, click the **Preview** button on the last page of the wizard. Use the player controls to run the video and then close the Web browser. Back in the **Recording Wizard**, click the **Finish** button. The Web page will be created and stored on your hard drive.

14 Publish the Page to the Web

Still in RealProducer, choose **Tools, Publish Web Page** to start the **Publishing Wizard**. This wizard will send the page you just produced to your Web server.

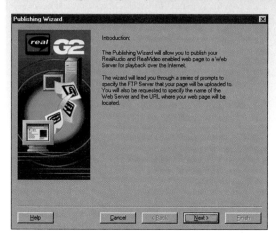

15 Choose the Web Page

Click **Next** and then click the **Browse** button to find the Web page you just created. Click **Next** again.

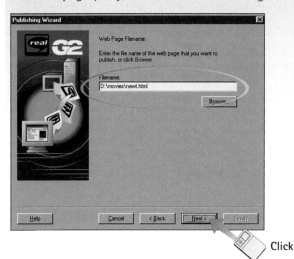

Click

16 Specify the Server Type

If you use one of the ISPs in the list, select it now. Otherwise, choose **Generic – No Defaults** and click the **Next** button.

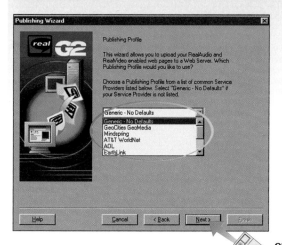

Click

17 Choose the Streaming Method

If you chose the **Generic** option, select the **Stream media clip from a standard Web server** option on this page and click **Next**. If you chose a specific service such as AOL, you will have to enter your username and password along with your assigned upload location and then click **Finish**. If you are using the **Generic** option, keep going to the next step.

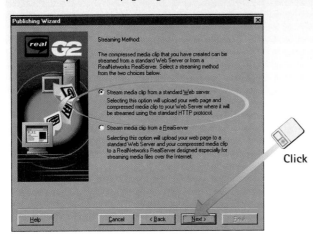

Click

18 Enter Server Data

Enter the location to which you plan to upload the Web page. Type the username and password for your Web page access and click **Next**.

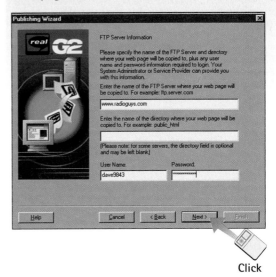

Click

19 Enter the URL

If the URL for your Web page is different than the location to which you are uploading the data, type the URL information now. Usually, however, you can accept the defaults on this page and just click **Next**.

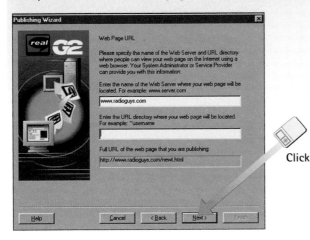

Click

20 Start the Upload

Click **Next** to upload the files that comprise your Web page to your Web site. When the upload process is complete, go to your Web page and experience the streaming video yourself.

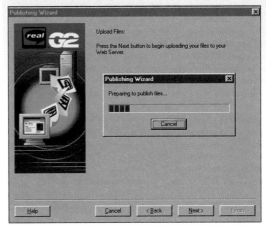

End

Task

PART 10

Incorporating Video into a PowerPoint Slide Show

*I*f you use PowerPoint to deliver presentations to students, co-workers, or clients, you might be excited to learn that it's a snap to add video clips to your shows. The same movies that you learned how to make earlier in this book can easily be added to any PowerPoint slide, which you can play during a presentation as an attention getter or to better describe a technique or process.

What do you need to add video to PowerPoint? First and foremost, some video. In this part of the book, I show you how to produce your finished video clips specifically for PowerPoint. You should also have a lot of hard disk space and a fairly fast PC. Remember that if you use a few video clips in your presentation, you will no longer be able to fit your PowerPoint show on a few floppy disks—it'll have to go on a laptop hard drive, CD-ROM, or Zip disk. Read on and see how it's all done. ●

How to Prepare Video for PowerPoint

By now you should know the drill—to put video into PowerPoint, you must first produce the movie. In other words, your raw footage must be rendered into a format that PowerPoint can display.

This is a good template for a video that will be included in PowerPoint.

You can edit these settings based on the specific PowerPoint presentation you're making.

Smart Video

Why would you want to use video in a PowerPoint presentation? For starters, don't use it just because you think a bright, shiny object will get you rave reviews. Instead, use video when it helps your presentation, as in these examples:

- Use video to demonstrate a technique.
- Use video to present a message from your CEO.
- Include a video clip to add ambiance to a presentation for the general public.

1 Start the Production

With your finished (and saved) video in the Storyline, it's time to produce the video. From the menu button, choose **Storyline, Produce**. The **Produce Movie** dialog box appears.

Click

2 Pick a Template

There are numerous templates you can choose for a PowerPoint presentation. The **Video-In-A-Window** template produces a nice, large video clip with excellent resolution, but you can experiment with others as well.

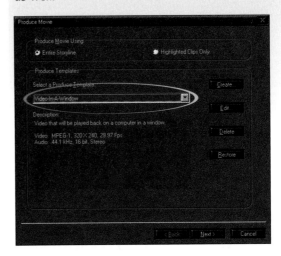

3 Edit the Settings

If you want to modify the video template, click the **Edit** button. In the **Settings** dialog box, you can change the video size, bit rate, and other factors. Note that if you switch to the MPEG-2 format, you can create much larger video windows.

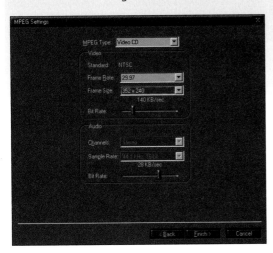

4 Produce the Video

Back in the **Summary Page**, click the **Produce** button; the video will be rendered to your hard drive in the AVI (Video for Windows) format. Don't be surprised if this step takes a while—perhaps even hours. You can track the video's progress onscreen. The file you have just produced is what you will add to PowerPoint in the next task.

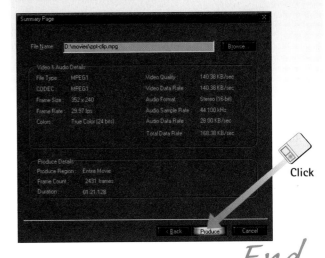

Click

End

How to Prepare Video for PowerPoint   223

How to Insert Video into PowerPoint

Now that your video has been prepared, it is time to add it to a PowerPoint presentation. After a few simple steps, you'll be ready to dazzle your audience with moving video in what is usually a fairly static slide show.

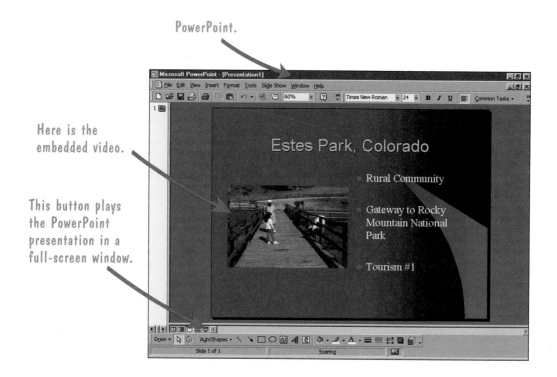

PowerPoint.

Here is the embedded video.

This button plays the PowerPoint presentation in a full-screen window.

Delivery Considerations

Before you add 100MB of video to your PowerPoint presentation, consider where and how you'll be delivering it. If the presentation is staying on your PC, that's fine. But if you need to copy the show to another PC, make sure that the entire show fits on a Zip disc or CD-ROM (if the system has a CD-RW drive). The last thing you need is to discover a half-hour before the big meeting that your 125MB presentation won't fit on a 100MB Zip disk.

Choose the Right Format

If you plan to deliver your presentation on a different computer, be sure to choose a common format such as MPEG-1 or AVI. If you render your movie in MPEG-2, it may not play on the final PC.

1 Add a New Slide

With PowerPoint running, you need to add a slide to your presentation. This is the slide to which you add the video. Choose **Common Tasks, New Slide** from the toolbar and double-click one of the slide templates that has a picture on it.

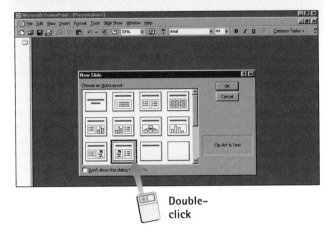

Double-click

2 Delete the Frame

I chose a slide with a picture on it because it's a great template for supporting a video window. We don't need the graphic frame, though, so click it and press the **Delete** key. You should now have just the title and text frames on the slide.

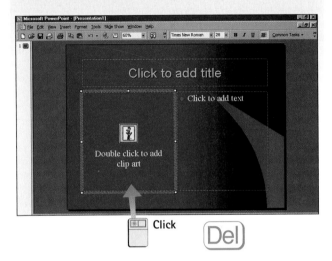

Click   Del

3 Insert the Movie

Choose **Insert, Movies and Sounds, Movie from File** from the menu. Locate the video you produced in VideoWave and click **OK**. You'll see a dialog box that asks whether you want the movie to play automatically in the slide show. The choice is up to you, but I recommend that you click **No** so that you can control when the movie starts.

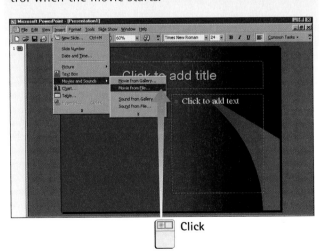

Click

4 Resize the Video

Use the sizing handles to resize the video window, and then click and drag within the video itself to move it around on the slide. Position and size the video window however you like; your video is now a part of your presentation.

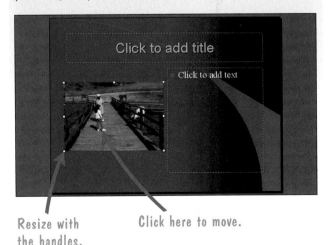

Resize with the handles.   Click here to move.

End

How to Play Video in PowerPoint

Videos add a splash of glitz to any presentation, and they can be truly useful as well. After you're running your presentation, you can play, stop, and restart videos with a few simple mouse clicks.

Right-click to see the control menu.

Here is the embedded video.

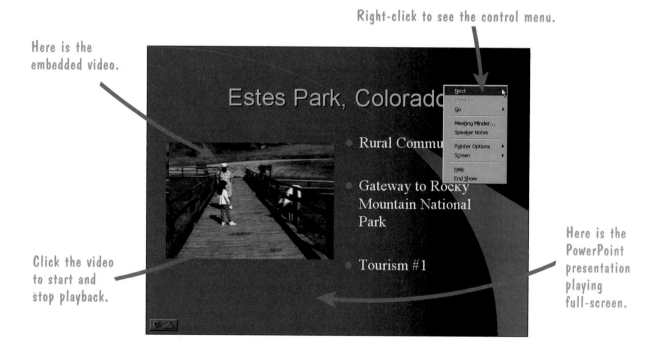

Estes Park, Colorado

Rural Commu

Gateway to Rocky Mountain National Park

Tourism #1

Click the video to start and stop playback.

Here is the PowerPoint presentation playing full-screen.

Effective Public Speaking

Video can brighten up your presentation, but you should also have some good speaking skills and deliver an otherwise polished presentation. I could write an entire book about presentation tips and tricks, but if you're hungry for some good stuff, check out *Small Business Microsoft Office 2000 for Dummies*, by Dave Johnson and Todd Stauffer. (Yeah, that was a plug for another book.)

1 Auto Play

When you added the video to PowerPoint (as described in the preceding task), you were given the option of allowing the movie to play automatically when you display the appropriate slide. If you chose **Yes**, the movie will start automatically.

2 Click to Play

If the movie does not start automatically when you display the slide, you must move the mouse pointer over the video window and click the mouse to start the video.

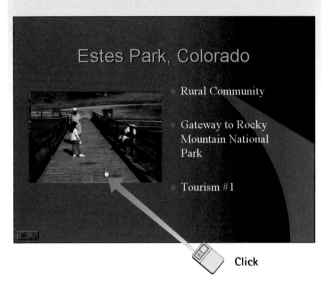

Click

3 Click to Pause

While the movie is playing, you can pause the action (to talk about what is happening, for example). To pause the video, move the mouse pointer over the video and click. Click the video again to restart the movie. You can pause and resume as often as you like.

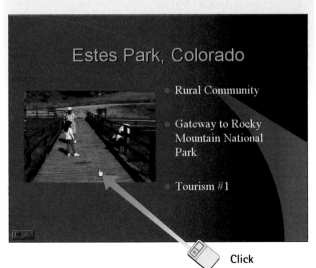

Click

4 Replay the Video

If you want to replay a video after it has completed, you have to redisplay the slide. To do that, right-click the slide (not the video) and choose **Go, By Title**; then reselect the same slide you're already on. You can then click the video to make it play.

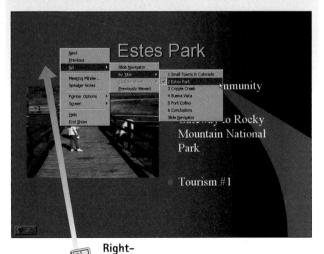

Right-click

End

Creating a PowerPoint Presentation with Video

PowerPoint is a great tool for developing and presenting slides with text, pictures, and small amounts of animation. You can also embed videos in your slides for extra punch. If you've read Part 10 of this book, you are already familiar with most of the steps

necessary to create a PowerPoint presentation with video. In this project, we'll go all the way and insert video, tweak the preferences, save the presentation, and hook your laptop up to a video system.

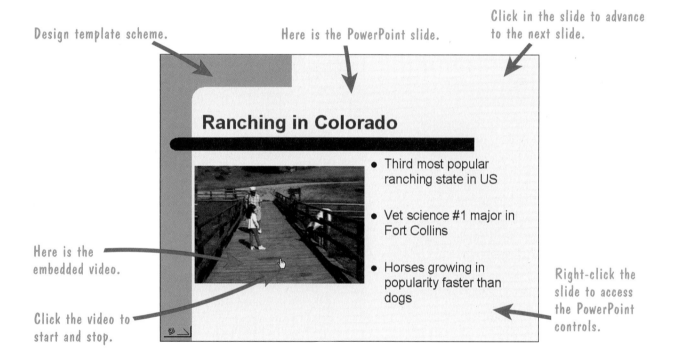

Design template scheme.

Here is the PowerPoint slide.

Click in the slide to advance to the next slide.

Here is the embedded video.

Click the video to start and stop.

Right-click the slide to access the PowerPoint controls.

Ranching in Colorado

- Third most popular ranching state in US
- Vet science #1 major in Fort Collins
- Horses growing in popularity faster than dogs

Your Video Properties

Most of the time, you want your PowerPoint videos to have the same properties. I recommend that you set them up this way:

- Usually, do not make clips loop indefinitely. Set them to play just once.

- Rewind the movie. When you set up the video to rewind automatically after it's done playing, you can play the video again without reloading the page.
- Don't set up the movie to play as soon as the page loads—usually, you want to control exactly when the movie starts.

1 Produce Your Video

The first step when creating a PowerPoint presentation with video is to produce any video clips you plan to include in the show. In VideoWave, choose **Storyline, Produce** from the menu button to open the **Produce Movie** dialog box.

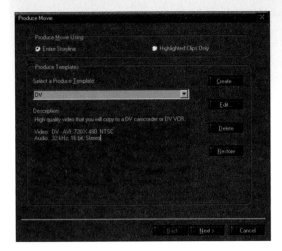

2 Pick a Template

As I mentioned in Part 10 of the book, the **Video-In-A-Window** template produces a nice, large video clip with excellent resolution—ideal for PowerPoint. If you want a larger video than the default, click the **Edit** button and fine-tune the settings.

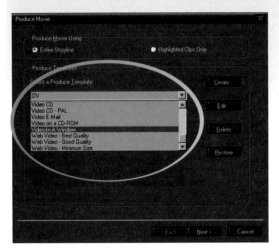

3 Produce It

When you're ready to make your clip, click the **Produce** button, located on the **Summary Page**. Wait while VideoWave generates your video and then save it to the hard drive. Produce all the movies you intend to embed in PowerPoint before moving on to the next step.

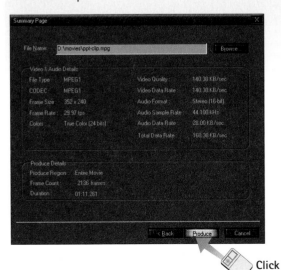

 Click

4 Start PowerPoint

Start PowerPoint; in the startup dialog box that appears, double-click the **Design Template** option to pick a custom look for your presentation.

 Double-click

continues

5 Pick a Design

Choose a design template from the **New Presentation** dialog box. If **Capsules** is available on your PC, select it and click **OK**. If that template doesn't exist on your computer, pick another (the **Capsules** template just happens to be one of my favorites).

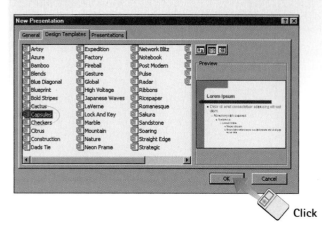

Click

6 Add a Title Slide

You'll see the **New Slide** dialog box. Because we want to add a title slide, click **OK** to accept the default options. Then enter a title and subtitle for your presentation by clicking in the appropriate text boxes and typing some appropriate text.

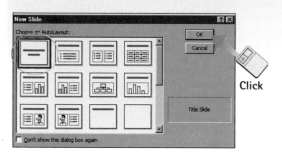

Click

7 Add a New Slide

Now add the slide on which your first video will appear. Choose **Common Tasks, New Slide** from the toolbar. From the **New Slide** dialog box, choose one of the slides that has a graphic side-by-side with text and click **OK**. The new slide loads onto the screen as shown here, ready for you to work with.

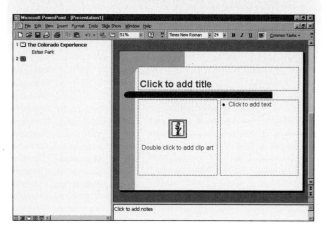

8 Add Text

Click in the text boxes and type to add a title for your slide as well as supplemental text. The text should support the video you are about to add to the side of the slide.

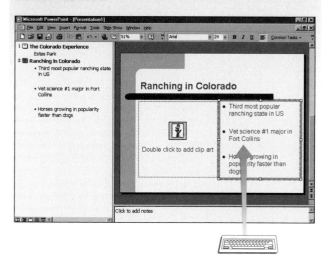

9 Delete the Graphic Frame

You don't really need the graphic frame; I chose this slide template because it's well designed to support video and text side by side. Click the frame for the graphic and then press the **Delete** key to remove it from the slide.

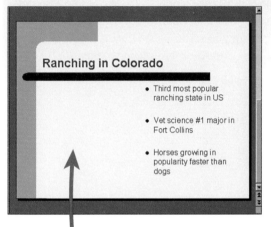

Remove the graphic frame.

10 Insert Your Video

Choose **Insert, Movies and Sounds, Movie from File** from the PowerPoint menu. Locate the video you produced in VideoWave and click **OK**.

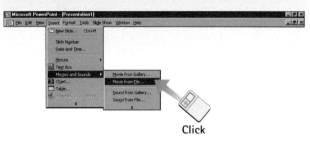

Click

11 Play Manually

A dialog box appears, asking whether you want the video to play automatically when the slide appears. You want it to play when you click it, so click the **No** button.

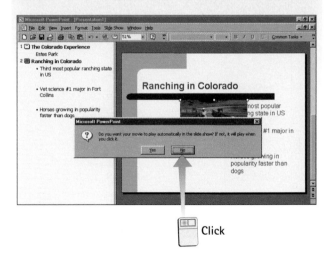

Click

12 Size and Position the Video

Drag the clip to the exact location on the slide where you want it to appear and resize it using the sizing handles. Size the video using only the corner handles, or you might accidentally change the video's proportions.

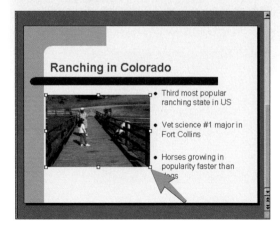

continues

13 View Movie Options

There are a few movie options you can tweak. To see the options, right-click the video and choose **Edit Movie Object** from the shortcut menu. The **Movie Options** dialog box opens.

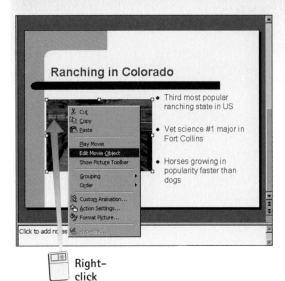

Right-click

14 Rewind the Movie

If you want to be able to play the movie more than once while running the presentation, select the **Rewind movie when done playing** option and click **OK**. Note that you can also make the movie play continuously by clicking **Loop until stopped**. I don't recommend that you loop the video because it's generally silly to have a video clip play over and over in a PowerPoint slide. You usually want it to play once and stop so that the presentation can continue.

Click

15 Add Other Slides

Your video is now embedded in a slide in the presentation. Choose **Common Tasks, New Slide** from the toolbar to open the **New Slide** dialog box and add other slides to your presentation. Finish by adding any other text and images to the presentation.

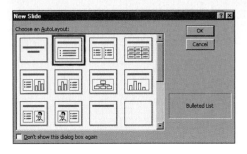

16 Save Your Work

Choose **File, Save As** from the menu and save your PowerPoint presentation with a meaningful filename. The file will be saved with a **.PPT** file extension.

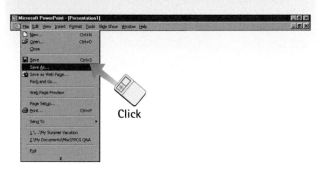

Click

17 Pack and Go

The video file is stored externally to your presentation file. That means that if you copy the presentation to a laptop or another PC to deliver the presentation, you must remember to copy the video file also. Although you can copy the files manually, an easier solution is to choose **File, Pack and Go** to start the **Pack and Go Wizard**. If you select the **Include linked files** option, PowerPoint can move all the files to another drive or PC for you.

18 Set Up the PC

If you're displaying the presentation on a computer screen, you're ready to go. But if you want to display the show on a projector screen or television, connect the video-out jack on the PC to the video system; connect the audio-out jack to a sound system.

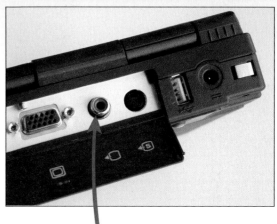

Video out.

19 Run the Slide Show

When you're ready to run the presentation, choose **Slide Show, View Show** from the menu. The presentation will start, and you can click the left mouse button to advance through your slides.

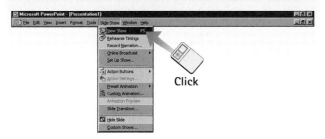

Click

20 Click to Play and Pause

When you encounter a slide with video, click the video window to start video playback. Click again to pause the video; click a third time to restart the paused video.

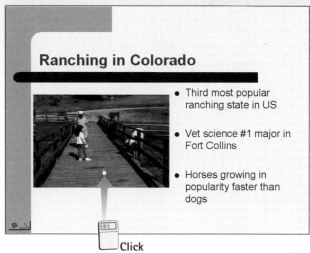

Click

End

Glossary

A

analog video Video captured by an older camcorder that uses a format such as VHS, S-VHS, 8mm, or Hi-8. These formats are all relatively low in overall video resolution and degrade with each copy that is made from the original source tape.

aperture setting The size of the opening that lets light through the lens to hit the film. The bigger the aperture's f/stop— expressed as f/2, f/5.6, or f/22, for instance—the smaller the aperture opening.

audio The portion of a recorded video file that provides the narration, music, or sound effects that accompany the visual portion of the film. Adding audio to your video can fill in the gaps and turn your simple video clips into a sophisticated multimedia presentation. Most video editors enable you to add several layers of video to your scenes in addition to the audio that was recorded on tape when you recorded the original scenes.

audio transition A technique in which the video transitions to a new scene aurally, not visually. For example, while watching the end of the first scene, you will hear the beginning of the next scene (such as a person's voice, street traffic, or a telephone) a few seconds before the second scene actually appears onscreen. Then the scene changes visually, and the audio is perfectly in synch with the visual.

B

backlight A light that is reflected off the background to add a sense of depth between the subject and the background.

bandwidth The amount of data that can be processed by a given device. An analog modem has very little bandwidth compared to a high-speed cable modem, for instance, and it cannot download video from the Internet nearly as quickly.

bit rate The speed at which a video file can stream from the Internet. When you create your streaming video file, you can control the bit rate at which the file will stream.

blue screen A specially colored backdrop that is later replaced with another video layer. For example, you can film your subject holding a blue screen (a uniquely colored board) that you will later edit to contain a second video.

BMP A file format used by Windows to display "wallpaper" images. The BMP format isn't practical for most applications because of the large file sizes associated with the format.

bug *See* watermark.

C

caption Text that labels a scene or identifies a location or person onscreen.

capture To put a moving image on a tape by using a video camera or camcorder. Also to transfer a video from a camcorder to the PC through a video card and using video editing software.

CCD An abbreviation for Charge Coupled Device, a CCD is a light-sensitive chip that acts like film in a traditional camera. The CCD renders the image projected through the lens, which is then written to videotape. The quality of a CCD is determined largely by its resolution, measured in pixels.

CD-Audio A high-quality sound format used by audio CDs that can be read and converted to other computer formats. VideoWave can read audio CDs, although Premiere cannot.

clip A short piece of video, sometimes called a scene. When creating a movie (or film or video project), you string together several clips that will play in sequential order to tell the "story" of your movie. The transitions between clips can help the progress of the movie as well.

color matte What Premier calls a *color panel*.

color panel A plain, single-color background you can use to start and end your video (or appear at any point within the video), display titles against, and do other special effects.

crawl When title text goes from left to right across the screen (or vice versa).

credit Text that tells who filmed, produced, and otherwise slaved over a film. Credits also identify who appeared in the film and what music you used. Watch a Hollywood movie all the way to the end for some ideas about who to include in your credits.

crop To make an image physically smaller by trimming away unwanted details. Cropping also reduces the size of the computer file.

cut To appear suddenly onscreen without any other kind of transition effect. The cut is the most basic kind of transition for changing scenes and dropping titles onto the screen.

D

depth of field The amount of the scene in front and in back of the focused subject that remains in focus. You can control the depth of field by adjusting the amount of zoom, shutter speed, or the aperture setting of the camera. Use depth of field to isolate the subject from the foreground and background or to keep the entire scene in focus.

digital image stabilization   A camcorder's digital attempt to reduce the apparent jitter or shakiness in a scene, especially when you're using the zoom.

digital video   Video that conforms to the new standards of DV, miniDV, or Digital8. These formats record video and audio as computer data is recorded, and are thus not subject to generational loss as is analog video.

digital zoom   A way of enlarging the image you see through the viewfinder (and record on film) using electronic trickery. Specifically, a digital zoom uses only the pixels in the middle of the CCD and enlarges them, often producing a noisy, grainy, and relatively ugly image. Avoid using the digital zoom very often—try to stay within the limits of the camera's optical zoom. *See also* optical zoom.

DIMM   The most common memory module in use among PCs today. DIMM stands for Dual Inline Memory Module.

dissolve   A video transition in which one video clip fades into the next.

dub   To make a copy from one tape (usually the master tape) to another tape.

E–F

f/stop   The aperture setting—that is, the size of the camera opening that lets light through to the film. The wider open the aperture, the smaller the f/stop setting value. For example, the most-open aperture for your camera may be f/2; when the aperture is shut down to its smallest diameter, the f/stop setting might be f/22.

face   The main, thick part of a text character.

fade   A video transition in which the scene "fades" from black or white into another scene.

fill light   A light that is reflected off another surface onto the subject. The reflector softens the effect of light on the subject.

focal length   The distance from the lens to the point behind the lens at which the rays of light focus and create an image. Typically, the longer the focal length of the lens, the higher its magnification. The focal length then also affects the overall look of your scene. A telephoto lens, for example, compresses the foreground and background while keeping only the subject in sharp focus. More moderate lens magnifications can keep everything in the scene in focus at the same time. Not all lenses have a fixed focal length; if you have a zoom lens, the focal length can actually change depending on the zoom's setting.

Foley effects   Special sound effects you can add to your video to suggest creaking doors, gunshots, and car engines, for instance.

freeze frame   A technique in which a particular frame of video is held onscreen. Sometimes the audio portion of the scene continues playing.

G

generational loss   The drop in video resolution that results when you make a copy of an analog videotape. The original videotape is called first generation; a copy of that is second generation, and so on.

GIF   A file format used in Web pages. GIF files can be made to display first in low resolution and then improve in quality as more data is downloaded.

grain   Texture on the film that occurs when there isn't enough light to make a good shot or when the camera uses its digital zoom. Grain usually refers to chemically processed film, but the digital equivalent of grain appears in video as well.

H–I

infrared recording   A feature that permits the camera to record images in absolute darkness using an infrared emitter. Sony Handycams have this feature, where it goes by the name **NightShot**. Infrared recording creates a greenish monochrome image similar to what you would see through night-vision goggles.

J

JPG   A file format that can compress huge photographic images into tiny file sizes while sacrificing only a little image quality. Great for Web pages and email.

K

key light   The main light in the room. It provides the principal light on the subject.

keywords   Descriptive words that help identify files on the Internet. Keywords can make it easier for Web surfers to find your video files in search engines.

L

leader   The beginning of the physical tape on a videocassette. The leader is a strip of nonrecording tape that connects the actual recording tape to the spindle on the cassette. Most cassette tapes have about five seconds of leader before the actual recording media portion of the tape begins.

lossless   Any file compression scheme that uses a nondestructive compression scheme and so does not degrade sound or video quality.

lossy A compression scheme for audio or video that actually destroys (hopefully) unimportant data to make the file smaller. Lossy compression schemes such as JPEG and MP3 try to eliminate information in subtle ways so that you aren't aware of the changes.

lux value A camera rating that indicates how low the light can be before the camera can no longer record an image. Lux values are subjective and are not standard, but typically a 2-lux camera can record an image in candlelight.

M

manual override To force the camera into different settings than those settings it would choose automatically. For example, you can manually override the exposure settings of most cameras, and you can trick the camera into focusing on something other than your subject. You override the camera's settings to achieve special effects.

Mark-In point The point in a longer video or audio clip at which you decide to start the clip. You can shorten a lengthy clip or "crop out" unwanted leading frames or noise by setting the Mark-In point. Keep in mind that when setting a Mark-In point, the beginning of the clip isn't physically deleted. Instead, the video editing software is smart enough to start playing the clip at the Mark-In point, which can be changed or deleted at any time during the movie production.

Mark-Out point The point in a longer video or audio clip at which you decide to stop the clip. You can shorten a lengthy clip or "crop out" unwanted trailing frames or noise by setting the Mark-Out point. Keep in mind that when setting a Mark-Out point, the end of the clip isn't physically deleted. Instead, the video editing software is smart enough to stop playing the clip at the Mark-Out point, which can be changed or deleted at any time during the movie production.

master The first tape you create from your PC video file, also known as the first-generation tape. The master tape is a high-quality source to which you should return whenever you want to make more copies. Although you could use the file on your hard drive as a master, you won't want to keep that file forever because it takes up so much storage space. If you're using analog video, however, the PC file is your master source and first generation; the first physical tape you record is considered to be a second-generation tape.

motion blur The effect of tracking a speeding object and thus blurring the background because of the motion of the camera.

MP3 A popular format for sound files. MP3 compresses the sound file so that it takes up less room on the hard disk and takes less time to upload or download to and from Web pages. The compression scheme does not affect sound quality noticeably; it's often just about CD quality. VideoWave reads MP3 files but Premiere does not.

N

narration A voice that explains what is happening on the video. A voiceover can add tremendous value to a video by explaining the situation being shown to viewers. You can do the narration on-scene when you film the video, but you'll generally get better results by recording the voiceover in a quiet studio (such as at your PC) and adding it to the video afterwards.

noise The random errors generated by your camcorder when filming in low-light situations. A camcorder's CCDs are designed to work with a certain minimum level of light; videotaping with less light results in the CCDs creating "phantom" pixels in the video that appear as noise.

O

optical zoom A way of enlarging the image you see through the viewfinder (and record on film) using the camera's optics. *See also* digital zoom.

outline The line that wraps around a text character—especially obvious with large, thick fonts.

overlay video When creating special effects with a blue screen, the clip that appears in the blue screen. The scene that surrounds the overlay (for example, the actor holding the blue screen on which the overlay video plays) is called the background video.

P

pixel A "dot" on the computer screen, usually used to describe image resolution. Every computer image is created from an array of pixels, usually 640×480, 800×600, or 1024×768 pixels.

plug-in A generic term for a special element you insert into a Web page. FrontPage uses the term to refer to any component (such as video) that needs a special viewer. When you want to include a video clip on your Web page, for example, the clip is called a plug-in to the Web page.

pop The annoying sound on a voice recording that accompanies an inexperienced narrator's pronunciation of certain letters. For example, many people blow out the letter *p*, which results in a *pop* when they speak into a microphone. You can minimize popping by varying your distance from the mike, changing the angle at which you speak into the mike, and using a foam cover on the mike.

produce To render a video production on your PC in its final form, storing it on your hard drive. The produced video becomes the high-quality master from which you can make any number of copies—and those copies will be every bit as good as the first copy.

Q-R

RealPlayer The standard playback software, distributed by Real Networks, for enjoying streaming media (such as audio and video) on the Internet.

RealProducer A free program that can be used to convert video into a Web-friendly streaming format. RealProducer is distributed by Real Networks to enable users to upload streaming video to the Internet easily and quickly.

reflector A card, fabric, or other reflective surface that you can use while shooting a scene to direct ambient light onto the subject. Reflectors are available at most photo and video stores, and they can dramatically enhance the quality of your film.

render *See* produce.

resolution The number of pixels used to display an image. Digital video cameras capture images at a resolution of 720×480 (720 pixels in a line by 480 lines). When printed, this resolution maintains the image's integrity only up to about 5×7 inches (good enough for Web pages and importing into Word or Publisher documents). For images with higher resolutions, you'll need a mega-pixel digital camera.

roll When title or credit text goes from the top to the bottom of the screen (or vice versa).

S

scale When printing an image, to reduce or enlarge by a specified percentage.

scene In VideoWave parlance, a clip that is already in the Storyline. The term "scene" is really just another way of describing a clip, and the two terms are frequently used interchangeably. *See also* clip.

script Text that identifies what everyone in the scene you are filming is going to say. The script can help you identify any weaknesses in the storyboard and also flesh out the video you are about to film.

SCSI A specification for ultra-high performance hard disks for the PC. It stands for Small Computer Serial Interface. SCSI has been largely supplanted by Ultra ATA/66, thanks to Ultra's lower cost and simpler setup.

shadow The optional backdrop that can make a text character stand out from the video background.

shutter speed The amount of time each frame of film is exposed to light.

SIMM An older kind of memory module still used by Pentium-based PCs. SIMM stands for Single Inline Memory Module.

slide *See* wipe.

still frame *See* freeze frame.

storyboard A series of cartoon-like panels you draw that describes, scene by scene, what happens in your movie. The storyboard can be either crudely drawn in pencil or elaborately produced on a computer. Regardless of how it is created, you'll find the storyboard handy for staying on track and on schedule.

storyboard template In VideoWave, a "dummy" video you can use to help structure your own video. If you need help organizing your film, open an appropriate storyboard from the `VideoWave\Media\Storyboard` folder. Each panel in the storyboard includes text that suggests a specific flow for your movie.

Storyline In VideoWave parlance, the set of panels that runs across the top of the screen. These panels contain individual video clips that, in the sequence presented, will become the video movie you are creating. You can think of the VideoWave Storyline as your movie's storyboard.

streaming video Video that plays onscreen even as it is being downloaded from the Internet to the viewer's PC. If the video file contains audio sounds, note that the audio portion of the clip streams right along with the video.

subtitle Onscreen text that translates foreign-language dialog or transcribes hard-to-understand speech.

T

talking head A film segment that shows just the head and shoulders of a person who is talking. This tight focus is often used in interview situations where the background is not as important as the talking subject is. It is also convenient in a movie destined for the Web, because the small amount of movement in a talking-head shot compresses well for the Internet.

TIF A file format that preserves all the image quality in a picture, although files can be huge.

title Text that can leap or fade or dance or spin its way onto the screen to identify your movie or specific scenes. Titles help your viewer immediately understand the context of your movie, and they add a professional touch to your production as well.

title case A capitalization convention in which the first, last, and all important words in the headline are given an initial capital letter. Most newspapers and magazines capitalize their headlines using title case; when you add titles to your videos, you should typically use this capitalization convention, too.

track To follow a moving subject with the camera lens.

transition A graphical segue that signals the end of one scene and the start of the next. The most basic transition is a cut: The first clip stops suddenly and the second clip begins without preamble. More artistic transition effects include fades, dissolves, and wipes in which the first clip somehow blends into the second clip.

U

Ultra ATA/66   A specification for one of the fastest kind of consumer hard disks currently available. An Ultra ATA/66 hard disk (and its associated hard disk controller) will ensure that you won't have any stutters or jitters in your video because of the drive. The only faster kind of hard disk that's generally available for PCs is a SCSI hard disk, but the additional performance offered by SCSI isn't worth the added complexity and expense.

V

voiceover   *See narration.*

W–Z

watermark   A small, semitransparent graphic that identifies a scene or speaker. Many TV broadcasts use a watermark to let you know what channel you're watching.

WAV   An older, but still popular, format for sound files. All video editors work with this lossless format. By default, VideoWave captures sound in the WAV format.

white balance   To adjust the camcorder so that it properly reproduces all the colors in your scene based on the available light. Because different light sources—such as daylight, florescent light, and candlelight—all generate different colors, they will cause all the colors in your scene to shift unless you compensate. White-balancing is a simple process in which you show your camcorder true white. When the camera knows what color white is, all the other colors come out accurately as well. Your camera usually adjusts for color balance automatically, but you can get better results by manually white-balancing your camcorder— especially indoors, in low-light situations, when using a camera light, or with unusually tinted overhead lights.

wipe   A video transition in which the new video physically moves into the frame while displacing the old video.

Index

CD-ROM Installation

Windows 95/NT/2000 Installation Instructions

1. Insert the CD-ROM disc into your CD-ROM drive.
2. From the Windows 95/NT/2000 desktop, double-click the My Computer icon. Some features might be accessible by right-clicking the CD icon from your My Computer menu.
3. Double-click the icon representing your CD-ROM drive.
4. Double-click the icon titled START.EXE to run the CD-ROM interface.

NOTE

If Windows 95/NT/2000 is installed on your computer, and you have the AutoPlay feature enabled, the START.EXE program starts automatically whenever you insert the disc into your CD-ROM drive.